HOW TO STUDY  Y

w/D

HOW TO STUDY
ROMANTIC
POETRY

Paul O'Flinn

HOW TO STUDY ROMANTIC POETRY

St. Martin's Press, Scholarly and Reference Division,
175 Fifth Avenue, New York, N.Y. 10010

First published in the United States of America in 2001

This book is printed on paper suitable for recycling and made from fully managed and sustained forest sources.

Printed in Malaysia

ISBN 0–333–92976–4

Library of Congress Cataloging-in-Publication Data

O'Flinn, Paul.
    How to study Romantic poetry / Paul O'Flinn.
        p.   cm. – (Study guides)
    Includes bibliographical references (p.) and index.
    ISBN 0–333–92976–4
        1. English poetry – 19th century – Examinations – Study guides.   2. English poetry – 19th century – Outlines, syllabi, etc.   3. Coleridge, Samuel Taylor, 1772–1834 – Examinations – Study guides.   4. Wordsworth, William, 1770–1850 – Examinations – Study guides.   5. Blake, William, 1757–1827 – Examinations – Study guides.   6. Keats, John, 1795–1821 – Examinations – Study guides.   7. Romanticism – England – Examinations – Study guides.   8. Romanticism – England – Outlines, syllabi, etc.   I. Title.   II. Series.
    PR590.O48   2000
    821'.709'071 – dc21   00-042058

CONTENTS

GENERAL EDITORS' PREFACE

EVERYBODY who studies literature, either for an examination or simply for pleasure, experiences the same problem: how to understand and respond to the text. As every student of literature knows, it is perfectly possible to read a book over and over again and yet still feel baffled and at a loss as to what to say about it. One answer to this problem, of course, is to accept someone else's view of the text, but how much more rewarding it would be if you could work out your own critical response to any book you choose or are required to study.

The aim of this series is to help you develop your critical skills by offering practical advice about how to read, understand and analyse literature. Each volume provides you with a clear method of study so that you can see how to set about tackling texts on your own. While the authors of each volume approach the problem in a different way, every book in the series attempts to provide you with some broad ideas about how to think about literature; each volume then shows you how to apply these ideas in a way which should help you construct your own analysis and interpretation. Unlike most critical books, therefore, the books in this series do not simply convey someone else's thinking about a text, but encourage you and show you how to think about a text for yourself.

Each book is written with an awareness that you are likely to be preparing for an examination, and therefore practical advice is given not only on how to understand and analyse literature, but also on how to organise a written response. Our hope is that, although these books are intended to serve a practical purpose, they may also enrich your enjoyment of literature by making you a more confident reader, alert to the interest and pleasure to be derived from literary texts.

John Peck
Martin Coyle

CHRONOLOGY

1757 Blake born, London.
1758 Robinson born, Bristol.
1759 Wollstonecraft born, Epping.
1764 Hargreaves invents spinning jenny.
1769 Watt patents steam engine.
1770 Estimated population of England and Wales: 7.48 million.
Wordsworth born, Cockermouth, Cumberland.
1772 Coleridge born, Ottery St Mary, Devon.
1774 Priestley discovers oxygen.
1775 Austen born, Steventon, Hampshire.
Robinson spends ten mouths in King's Bench Prison.
1776 American Declaration of Independence.
1779 Crompton invents spinning mule.
1780 Gordon Riots: Blake at the burning of Newgate Prison.
1783 Treaty of Versailles: American independence recognised.
1785 Cartwright invents power loom.
Yearsley, *Poems on Several Occasions*.
1787 American Constitution signed.
1788 Byron born, London.
1789 Fall of the Bastille: French Revolution begins. Blake, *Songs of Innocence*.
Hands, *The Death of Amnon* (includes 'On An Unsociable Family').
1790 Estimated population of England and Wales: 8.68 million.
1791 Paine, *Rights of Man*, Part One.
1792 Royal Proclamation Against Divers Seditious Publications. Paine outlawed.
Continental allies invade France. September massacres in Paris.
Shelley born, Warnham, Sussex.
Paine, *Rights of Man*, Part Two.
Blake, *The Marriage of Heaven and Hell*.
Wollstonecraft, *A Vindication of the Rights of Woman*.
1793 Louis XVI executed. Britain and France at war. The Reign of Terror.

Godwin, *Enquiry Concerning Political Justice.*
Wordsworth, 'Reply to the Bishop of Llandaff'.
1794   Trial and acquittal of Holcroft, Thelwall and Tooke.
Blake, *Songs of Innocence and of Experience.*
1795   Robinson, 'January, 1795'.
Seditious Meetings Act and Treasonable Practices Act.
Keats born, London.
1796   Coleridge, *Poems on Various Subjects* (including 'The Eolian Harp').
1797   Coleridge writes 'Kubla Khan'.
Wollstonecraft dies.
1798   Wordsworth and Coleridge, *Lyrical Ballads.*
Polwhele, 'The Unsex'd Females'.
1799   London Corresponding Society suppressed.
Combination Acts make unions illegal.
Napoleon assumes absolute power as First Consul.
Wordsworth completes two-part *Prelude.*
Robinson, *A Letter to the Women of England.*
1800   Britain produces over 80 per cent of world's coal and over 40 per cent of pig iron.
Wordsworth, Preface to *Lyrical Ballads*, second edition.
Robinson dies.
1802   Peace of Amiens (March): brief interlude in Anglo-French war.
First practical steamship launched on Clyde.
1803   Anglo-French war resumes.
1804   Napoleon becomes Emperor.
Blake tried for sedition and acquitted.
1805   Battle of Trafalgar.
Wordsworth completes second version of *The Prelude.*
1810   Cobbett imprisoned for two years for attacking the use for flogging in the army.
1811   Population of England and Wales: 10.16 million.
First attacks by Luddites in Nottinghamshire.
1812   Tory Prime Minister Spencer Perceval murdered.
1813   Leigh Hunt imprisoned for two years for libelling the Prince Regent.
Southey Poet Laureate.
Wordsworth Distributor of Stamps for Westmorland.
1814   Napoleon abdicates.
Stephenson's locomotive.
Wordsworth, *The Excursion.*

1815   Battle of Waterloo. End of Anglo-French war.
       Restoration of Louis XVIII.
1816   Coleridge, *Christabel, Kubla Khan, Pains of Sleep.*
1817   Habeas Corpus suspended.
       Coleridge, *Biographia Literaria.* Keats, *Poems.*
1818   Keats starts *Hyperion* and publishes *Endymion.*
1819   Peterloo Massacre. 'Six Acts' severely limit the freedom of the
       press and the right to demonstrate.
       Keats starts *The Fall of Hyperion* and writes 'La Belle Dame sans
       Merci' and his six major odes.
1820   Keats, *Lamia, Isabella, Eve of St Agnes and Other Poems.*
1821   Population of England and Wales: 12 million.
       Napoleon dies.
       Keats dies.
1822   Foreign Secretary Castlereagh commits suicide.
       Shelley dies.
1824   Byron dies.
1827   Blake dies.
1834   Coleridge dies.
1850   Wordsworth dies. The final version of *The Prelude* published.

INTRODUCTION: UNDERSTANDING ROMANTIC POETRY

I

MOST people reading a book of this kind nip through the preliminary sections as quickly as possible. Title page, list of contents, acknowledgements ('. . . thanks above all to my wife, but for whose tireless work typing the manuscript and strangling the dog, this book would never . . .') are usually dull or condescending or both, and a bit like the wrapping on a Christmas present – irritating bits of tinsel that get in the way of the real business and hence need to be disposed of as fast as decently possible. If you have taken that understandable route and arrived at this point by slipping past the chronological table at the start, please go back and browse through it for a bit That list of dates is not routine, surplus wrapping but crucial to an understanding of Romantic poetry.

What a glance at the table will tell you is that Romantic poetry gets written during a period of wars and of revolutions, a period of changes at once profound, frightening and exciting as human society reorganised itself at every level. In some senses, of course, that is always true: everyone's granny usually and rightly insists that things were different back in her day. However, what is unique about the Romantic period, which normally means the half century from about 1780 to about 1830, is the extent and depth of those changes. It is, for example, the time when Britain underwent the world's first industrial revolution and so emerged with an economy and a class formation more radically reconstructed than in any other half century in British history. That in turn eventually meant different work habits, different leisure patterns, different prospects and even different sex lives for most people in these islands. At the same time, the French Revolution and the American War of Independence changed the way those countries were governed, and at once made old certainties seem questionable and new possibilities seem feasible for everyone else.

It used to be common in literary studies to describe facts of this sort as 'background information'. They were disposed of in a first chapter, probably indeed called 'The Historical Background', which most readers skipped smartly over in pursuit of the more important bits where the author actually started talking about the poems. Once you call something 'background' you invite this sort of response, because it suggests something remote and unfocused and not part of the important foreground. But if you think of the way you and indeed the poets we shall be looking at in this book live your lives, then you will see at once that things do not separate themselves out in that trite way. When you or anyone sits down to write, then it is out of exactly those large and pressing experiences and the way they mould your life that you speak if you want to say something significant.

I am not trying to argue that Romantic poetry in some direct and straightforward way tells us about, for example, the French Revolution and hence is a useful source of data for history students. Rather, the argument is that, without some basic grasp of the context that surrounds and shapes Romantic texts, those texts can often mean very little. Such a grasp helps us to understand from the beginning what, in the broadest sense, a text is about, because we know something of the particular tensions, hopes and fears that informed it.

From the start I should like to underline this idea of tensions, hopes and fears, because it is out of that complex of emotions that most of the best Romantic poetry gets written. So a way into those poems is to search for the point of tension in them. In the poems we shall look at in the following chapters this tension comes in various guises. It begins as an understandable response to a turbulent, distressing and exhilarating history which formed and cut across the poets' lives from various directions and in complicated ways. And, then, what happens in the poetry is not a simple reflection of that history and the tensions, hopes and fears it generated, but rather we see the poets taking hold of the experience, exploring and negotiating it, using the full resources of language to make something new out of it, but a something new that is still constituted by the materials that the poets bring to the poem from their own lives and their own history. That making of poetry takes two major forms in the Romantic period: lyric and narrative. But always, with both forms, in order to understand the poems we shall need to move back to a context that informs the text and then forward to the way that context is reshaped and agonised into a particular poem.

It follows that an informed reading of a poem will need to begin with a working grasp of the history out of which the poem emerges and to which it addresses itself. But that does not mean that you have to be familiar with, say, the development of the textile industry in the late eighteenth century before you can read Wordsworth's 'Michael'. What it does mean, though, is that poems that can initially appear baffling or pointless can begin to make sense if you can learn to see them as part of a particular moment with its distinctive preoccupations, claims and feelings.

II

There are two ideas that it is essential to hold on to from the start. The first is that you need to think of Romantic literature not as escapist in the way the term 'Romantic' sometimes suggests, but as literature that tries passionately to come to terms with the modern world as it emerges through a series of wrenching changes. And secondly you have to be aware that, because those changes affected men and women, working class and middle class, north and south and so on in different ways, what we get in the literature of the period is a range of competing, arguing, contending voices rather than a series of common assumptions that all share and that can be neatly summarised. Let us look at these two claims in a bit more detail.

First, then, 'Romantic'. Say the word and what do you think of? Something dreamy and remote – impossibly idealised versions of love, perhaps, vaguely glimpsed through Barbara Cartland's veils while violins scrape somewhere in the background. Or, if you move a bit closer to easily available notions of Romantic literature, the term still carries much the same connotations: the first thing that comes to mind maybe is an unfortunate picture of Keats looking a wistful wimp or Wordsworth maundering on about daffodils; Shelley flits past with too much hair but not much practical skill when it comes to paying the bills; over there lies Coleridge, stoned out of his mind, while in the corner Blake is talking to the fairies.

Against these superficial images we need to place some facts. In 1795 Coleridge lectured against the Government's war policy and was the target of Government spying. In 1798 Wordsworth and his sister Dorothy were driven out of Alfoxden because of neighbours' suspicions of their radical politics. In 1804 Blake was put on trial for sedition and avoided a long prison sentence because of the common sense of an English jury rather than the compassion of the English judiciary. In 1813 it seems that a Government spy tried to murder Shelley. In 1824 Byron died in exile in Missolonghi while fighting for Greek independence. And if you look at writers other than these major Romantic poets you come up with more of the same turbulence. The future essayist and Poet Laureate Robert Southey was expelled from Westminster School in 1792 for writing an article against corporal punishment. The journalist William Cobbett was imprisoned for two years between 1810 and 1812 for his criticism of the flogging of militiamen and then put on trial for sedition in 1831, while another journalist and friend of Keats, Leigh Hunt, was imprisoned for two years between 1813 and 1815 for libelling the Prince Regent. The writer Tom Paine was declared an outlaw for penning *Rights of Man* in 1792. He settled in revolutionary France and there he met an old friend, Mary Wollstonecraft, author of *A Vindication of the Rights of Woman*, which scandalised conservative opinion when it was published in 1792. Also part of that group of writers in France was the poet Helen Maria Williams who became a French citizen in 1817.

Of course there was more to the lives of these people than this selective list of incidents conveys, and some of them – for example, Wordsworth and Southey – certainly became depressingly reactionary in later years. But what those incidents (and the list could be considerably extended) suggest is a group of men and women who were certainly not 'Romantic' in any escapist or trivial sense but who on the contrary challenged dominant contemporary values and chose to use their pens not to doodle prettily in the margins of life but to probe and dissect at the heart of things. And they did it to the profound annoyance of the authorities, not to mention most contemporary reviewers and readers of poetry.

It is this brave thinking and writing that makes Romantic literature still exciting reading, and it is reading that is all the more powerful because it speaks about a world that we not only recognise but also still inhabit. If you glance again at the dates in the chronological table at the beginning, you can see behind those bald facts the cultural, political and economic structures of the modern world being laid down by three revolutions – American, French and Industrial. The American Revolution had started in 1776 when the thirteen colonies had declared their independence from Britain, and ended after seven years of war with British recognition of that independence in 1783. Nine years later you can still smell the excitement of the venture when one of the chief theorists of the struggle, Tom Paine, concludes *Rights of Man* by rubbing his hands and cheerfully declaring as he anticipates the imminent collapse of reactionary governments across Europe, 'It is, however, not difficult to perceive that the spring is begun. Thus wishing, as I sincerely do, freedom and happiness to all nations, I close the second part.'

The fall of the Bastille in July 1789 is the moment when the French Revolution struck British consciousness and from most sensible people the reaction was unmixed delight. Coleridge was only sixteen at the time and celebrated the event soon afterwards in 'Destruction of the Bastille'. Reading the poem now we can get a powerful sense of the inspiration flowing from that watershed in European history in spite of the naïveté of the expression:

Yes! Liberty the soul of Life shall reign,
Shall throb in every pulse, shall flow thro' every vein!

Successive events – Britain's war with France beginning in 1793, the Reign of Terror in 1793–4, Napoleon's coup in 1799 – confused and dissolved a lot of that early support, but more than a generation later the French Revolution, its possibilities and its failures, remained the starting point when Shelley set about drawing up an agenda for human liberation in *Prometheus Unbound*. And this although Britain was at war with France for nearly all of Shelley's life and indeed for the bulk of the Romantic period. The war that commenced in 1793 lasted with only a brief break in 1802–3 till 1815, and the suffering and the passion erupting from that conflict cascades across the literature of those years.

Nearly ten generations after the Industrial Revolution we are still struggling to come to terms with the way it changed the world, and the impact for that first generation must have been depressing, terrifying and intoxicating to a scarcely bearable degree. Imagine, for example, a place such as Manchester changing from an overgrown village of 27,000 people with no cotton mills in 1773 to a town of 95,000 with more than fifty mills in 1802 – imagine for a moment how it would feel to live and work through that monstrous change, quite unprecedented in human history, and you begin to understand some of the responses. Responses as apparently trivial as shifts in the language to accommodate new notions of class instead of customary ones such as

rank, and responses as angry as those of the Luddites who across the
north of England between 1811 and 1816 fought to defend a traditional livelihood and culture by smashing the machines that were used
to impoverish them. And yet imagine the possibilities too. The Industrial Revolution meant that for the very first time the great mass of
people were no longer necessarily condemned to a life of brute labour
just to avoid starving, to a life constantly at the mercy of natural dis-
asters and diseases. The huge increase in the productivity of labour that
was at the centre of the Revolution opened up, at least in theory, the
chance of leisure and recreation, of education and self-development for
everyone rather than for just a tiny, threatened and threatening elite as
always in the past. The savage, systematic denial of that chance by the
authorities and the economic structure they presided over did not stop
Shelley, for example, from elaborating a vision of human beings set free
by the new technologies and their own struggles in Act IV of *Prometheus
Unbound*.

My point is that great Romantic poetry does not turn its back on all
these shattering changes and wander off up an Alp to sniff flowers and
contemplate eternal verities. It is true that for the most part the poets
do not speak directly about those events, although they do sometimes:
the French Revolution, for example, is unsurprisingly the subject matter
of Blake's poem *The French Revolution* and also of books IX, X and XI
of Wordsworth's *The Prelude*. But they always speak out of the tensions,
hopes and fears of living in that era. That set of feelings can drive them
in a variety of directions: off, for example, to the past with a new sense
of it as fascinatingly different from the present, as in Keats's 'The Eve
of St Agnes'; of forward into the extravagant fantasies about future possibilities that we find in Blake's prophetic books; or, in Wordsworth's
poetry, out into the countryside with a painfully sharpened sense of its
beauty as creeping brick and smoke begin to smother it; or back deep
into the sort of anxious scrutiny of an inner self under strange pressures
that spurs Coleridge into writing 'The Ancient Mariner'; or, again and
again, into verse filled with radical idealism inspired by or angrily
pressed against the rapidly changing reality the poets saw and felt all
round them. But always at the core of these very different poems is the
same prompting and stubbornly unavoidable history.

While all of this is true, we need to pause here for a moment and
qualify that truth by going back to the second important idea I raised
at the start of this section – namely, the fact that, because the vast shifts
of the years 1780 to 1830 hit different people in different ways, what
we get in the literature is a range of voices saying different, often con-

tradictory things rather than some abstract and meaningless Spirit of the Age saying the same things again and again. I think you can grasp this point most easily if you think briefly of our own time rather than two hundred years ago. A historian in the future looking back at us might be tempted to say things like 'The British people in the late 1990s believed that . . .', or 'at the start of the twenty-first century Britain felt that . . .', but we who live in these times know that to talk in that way is a distortion to the point of being a lie. For, after all, what are the feelings and beliefs that a prosperous stockbroker in Guildford shares with a sacked miner in Doncaster? And what do they both share with a Welsh Nationalist in Llanelli or a pensioner in Wapping? Not a lot, probably. True, they all live in the same country at the same time, but what it offers them and their responses to it are radically contrary – now as in the Romantic period.

For the major Romantic poets were as diverse a group of individuals as those of our contemporaries I have just mentioned. Keats was born over a livery stable, the Swan and Hoop, in north London, whereas Shelley was born on the family estate at Field Place, Warnham, in Sussex. Byron was a Cambridge graduate, whereas Blake never went to school. Coleridge was a life-long Christian, whereas Keats was an atheist. Byron was an aristocrat, whereas Keats was sometimes sneered at as a Cockney. Blake was in lodgings in Soho at a time when Shelley was lodging at a palace in Pisa. The government that tried Blake for sedition was the same government that appointed Wordsworth Distributor of Stamps for Westmorland. Coleridge was the son of a vicar and thought about becoming a minister himself in a church that Blake angrily dismissed as a conspiracy against the people. I could go on, but the point I hope is made. The Romantic poets were certainly faced by a common set of problems, by a world slipping and sliding alarmingly beneath their feet, but they came to it from radically different directions and they clung on in radically different ways. For example, Wordsworth produced well over a hundred Ecclesiastical Sonnets, whereas Keats had better things to do than bother with what he scorned in an 1819 letter as 'the pious frauds of Religion'.

So where does that get us? Well, it means you should treat with deep suspicion any statement beginning 'Romantic poetry stresses', or 'Romantics thought that', convenient though such phrases seem for the hard-pressed student trying to rake some notions together the night before an exam. Instead, approach the problem differently: set out with a rough, working sense of the time and the place and then ask yourself what *this* text – written, perhaps, by an atheist or a Unitarian, a lord or an unemployed engraver, a Cockney or a northerner – does with those circumstances. What is the specific contribution that *this* poem makes to the disparate, fragmentary, sprawling bulk of Romantic literature? That way at least you get to see the poem plain instead of burying it under a heap of generalisations about Romanticism which, as we have seen, are usually of doubtful worth.

III

It was easy enough for me to sit here and type out the suggestion in the last paragraph. But the real problem is how to carry it out, how to tackle and make sense of an unfamiliar poem. In Chapters 2 and 4 I shall outline a method for working on lyric and narrative poems, but, before getting down to that, an idea worth grasping from the start is the notion of *choice and combination*.

Simply, when producing a poem, a writer *chooses* one word rather than another and then *combines* that choice with others and so builds up the poem. Of course, this is no profound insight into the mystery of poetic composition, because it is a process that all of us go through every time we use words. We do it rapidly and fairly unthinkingly when we chat casually to a friend, but in a more considered way when, for example, we write an essay or a job application. In poetry, which uses language to the limits of its capacity, stretching it here to reach for a new meaning, condensing it there to produce a more powerful impact, this process of choice and combination is painfully and carefully worked over, and most poems go through several drafts before the poet is even half satisfied that it has come out right. The three economical stanzas of Wordsworth's lyric 'She Dwelt among the Untrodden Ways', for instance, began as five much looser ones including such trite lines as 'Her lips were red as roses are'. Blake's powerful opening to 'London'. –

> I wander thro' each charter'd street,
> Near where the charter'd Thames does flow

– read, in an earlier version,

> I wander thro' each dirty street,
> Near where the dirty Thames does flow.

The earlier version constructs in the reader's mind a significantly different image of the city from the one Blake settled on. 'Dirty' is a straightforward description of the physical appearance of the place, but the repeated 'charter'd' should start us thinking about the charters of London, about the organisation, ownership and control of the capital – about the sort of political and social issues, in other words, that the rest of the poem goes on to develop.

We can trace these changes because in these two cases the early drafts survive. Usually they do not, but the point of the examples still stands. In every poem the words have been very carefully chosen to conduct us in particular directions, to inspire in us this emotion rather than that, to suggest one idea rather than another, to make these specific connections rather than those. So, one way to understand a poem is to stop and think about those directions, emotions and connections for a bit. What is this poem highlighting? What is the main idea that is being constructed and what particular terms go to make it up? Where am I, the reader, being guided? Where are the choices and combinations sending me? Once you begin to look at poems in that way – and I shall give several examples in the following chapters – then you can start to talk relevantly and purposefully about them.

IV

What I have tried to do in this opening chapter is to avoid setting up a series of big generalisations about Romantic poetry, because I think they block your view of the poems themselves, so that you are forced in the end to reproduce the generalisations rather than talk about the poems. Instead, I have suggested that you learn to see the period from 1780 to 1830 as one of more or less permanent wars and as marked by three large revolutions – American, French and Industrial – that painfully hacked out the modern world. Try to see it as an era that provoked in the poets we shall be looking at in this book a disparate cluster of tensions, hopes and fears that was central to their outlook when they sat down to write. How those tensions, hopes and fears express themselves in the resulting poems is through the process of choice and combination, because it is in that process of picking and choosing, highlighting and discarding, joining and constructing that poets betray their particular visions to the reader and try to set up in the reader a similar way of experiencing and seeing the world. So in reading those poems now we need to start by looking for the broad idea. Then listen carefully to the special emphases introduced into that idea by the poem and its terms, seeing what words have been used and what sort of associations they call up, how they highlight certain aspects and join them together with others, to produce in the reader a distinctive set of emotions and reactions. To take a simple example: in Blake's 'Holy Thursday' lyric in *Songs of Experience* he describes the hand that feeds the children from the charity orphanages as 'cold and usurous'. There are lots of ways you can describe a hand: 'pink and gummed up with rhubarb jam' is the way I would describe my daughter's hand right now. Blake knew all of those words; they were all at his disposal. Why did he choose 'cold and usurous' instead? How do those terms make us think of the people who funded the orphanages?

It is clearly time to look a bit more closely at Blake and his work.

2

STUDYING A BLAKE POEM

I

THE PLACE where most people start their study of Blake's poetry is the collection called *Songs of Innocence and of Experience*, first published in 1794, although *Songs of Innocence* had been issued on its own in 1789. Before looking closely at the poems, and to avoid grasping vainly at them in a vacuum, we need to have some idea of the man who produced them.

William Blake was born in Soho in 1757. The family lived on his father's slender earnings as a hosier. At the age of fourteen Blake began a traditional seven-year apprenticeship to an engraver, James Basire. In 1780 he was involved in the Gordon Riots, which burst out as anti Catholic disturbances but which soon swept up other grievances, and Blake was one of those who watched Newgate Prison burn to the ground. Two years later he married Catherine Boucher, a market gardener's daughter from Battersea. For a while, around the time of the composition of *Songs of Innocence and of Experience*, he was part of the group of radical thinkers and writers who met at the home of the publisher Joseph Johnson – people such as Tom Paine, the philosopher William Godwin and the feminist Mary Wollstonecraft. But that circle had broken up by the mid 1790s as the Government set about silencing the opposition, and the rest of Blake's life is the story of a not very successful attempt to earn a living as an engraver, painter and illustrator. All of it was spent in London except for the years 1800–3 when he had a frustrating spell at Felpham in Sussex trying to work under the dictates of a patron, William Hayley. It was during his stay at Felpham

that Blake had a vigorous argument with a dragoon and was charged
with having 'uttered seditious and treasonable expressions'. He was
acquitted in 1804 and passed his remaining years in relative obscurity
till his death in 1827.

So what is the relevance of those dry facts to *Songs of Innocence and of
Experience*? Well, they tell us quite a lot about what sort of poet Blake
was. His father was not, say, a vicar or a member of one of the middle-
class professions; Blake himself did not go to a public school or to
Oxford or Cambridge; he did not have a private income or easy access
to money-lenders prepared to subsidise him on the basis of comfortable
expectations. All of those things made him different from the average
eighteenth- or nineteenth-century poet. He came to poetry from a
different direction – from the artisan classes of London – with different
hopes, different experiences, different pressures from those of most of
the poets you might meet in standard syllabuses. Unsurprisingly, therefore, he wrote very different poetry.

To start with, he produced it in a very different way. Most poets send
their work off to a publisher and that is the last they see of it till it
appears in a bookshop, designed, printed and distributed by someone
else. Blake, by contrast, did all of those things himself, with Catherine's
help in the case of the *Songs*. He composed the poems, etched them onto
copper plates with the illuminations that accompany them, coloured in
those illuminations with Catherine's assistance, and then sold the work
himself. Blake, in short, was completely in control of the end product,
not subject to the whims of a publisher, the prejudices of an editor or
the market pressures of a bookseller. It was a radical way of doing things
and gave him room to write some radical poems.

If we turn, therefore, to those poems in the *Songs of Innocence and of
Experience*, the first thing we might note about them is that they are all
lyrics. 'Lyric' is one of those words that in a sense we all understand
because it is a familiar part of the pop culture that surrounds us, and so
there is a temptation to move past it without much thought. But, if we
are to understand some of the things that Romantic poetry tries to do,
then it is a term we need to stop and think about for a while. If we have
a notion of what the lyric as a form is designed to achieve, then we can
read an example of it with some idea of what to look for and what to
expect. The poet, after all, takes a decision to organise her or his writing
in one way rather than another, and we ought to keep that decision and
its implications in mind if we want to make sense of the resulting poem.

Poetry can be broadly subdivided into two forms, narrative and lyric.
Both subdivide further: odes and sonnets, for instance, are lyrics, and
we shall look at some examples of them in later chapters. But to start

with we can say that one of the primary aims of a narrative poem is to tell a story, whereas a lyric sets out to do other things. The lyric may briefly describe a slight incident or experience, but its primary interest is in the impact of that moment on the poet's own thoughts and feelings. The presentation of those thoughts and feelings is what a lyric poem is for, what it is designed to do. What we get, then, in a lyric is not a lengthy working-out of a philosophy of life or the unfolding of a complex plot but the capturing of a particular moment and, above all, the mood or insight it stimulated in the poet. The focus is on that private mood and that personal insight, and this is why the author chooses the lyric form in the first place. If you think about it you will see that this sort of unblurred focus is much more difficult in, for example, a story or an essay where other things are going on and where readers bring other expectations and demands. (The reader of an essay, to take one instance, might legitimately expect careful argument backed by substantial evidence, whereas it is pointless to demand that from a lyric.) If you want to explore the emotions and ideas that some incident has provoked in you, then you write a lyric, because right from its origins in ancient Greece that is what the form has been for. There, 'lyric' meant 'poetry sung to the lyre' (the lyre being a small stringed instrument like a harp) and was the form where the poet had freedom to deal with her or his feelings about anything from love to frogs. In this it differed from forms such as epic and drama, where the audience's expectations were for larger, more impersonal themes such as matters of religion or national history. Blake alludes to this original meaning of lyric by titling his volume *Songs*.

It is a statistical fact about the literature of the Romantic period that proportionately more lyrics were written during that era than in the immediately previous one, and you can check that by flipping through a standard anthology such as *The Oxford Book of Eighteenth-Century Verse*. There you can see easily enough the dominance in the early part of the century of other types of poem, such as the classical imitation or translation, the epigram, the pastoral and the satire. Why that shift to the lyric occurred is obviously one of those large questions about dislocations and shifts of direction in a culture whose full investigation would take more time and space than we have here. But what it clearly enough indicates is a deeper interest on the part of both poets and their readers with the inner workings of the self, with all those quirky, startling, disturbing little flickers that blink for a moment inside the mind and heart of the individual as he or she moves through the day.

It is quite legitimate to link this new centre of attention to that series of revolutions described in the previous chapter. They offered, as we saw, greater restraints but also greater possibilities to most individuals than any previous generation in human history. If the world around you appeared to be crumbling and re-forming itself with terrifying speed, one obvious response might be to draw back from its confusion and lack of certainty into the things you could be sure of – namely, your own hopes and fears, – and this is a move we shall see happening in some of the poems we shall look at. Equally, in other poems we shall see those revolutions, involving as they did the sweeping-away of traditional authorities and the substitution of new ideas about democracy and the rights of the individual, prompting writers to examine that individual – the poet – with a fresh sense of her or his worth and the importance of the individual's intuitive moments. The lyric appeared for the first time in ancient Greece, which saw humanity's first wobbling steps towards democracy; it is no accident that the form revived sharply in an age when those steps began to echo again and the individual stood up against priest and king.

II

So where does that leave us? Well, I hope by this stage you have some idea who Blake was and some ideas about lyric poetry. The time has come to take the next step and suggest a method for actually reading those poems. The method involves four simple steps; I shall start by outlining them and then show them at work on a couple of poems from *Songs of Innocence and of Experience*. As you go on with your studies you will perhaps want to sophisticate the method a bit, adding an extra concept here or a fresh guideline there, but in general I think you will find it supplies a useful rule of thumb for directing you towards what matters in a text. I hope at least that it saves you from that panicky feeling, which everyone who has ever written an exam knows only too well, of desperately looking for something substantial to say.

Here, then, are those four steps.

I   Read the poem through slowly at least twice and look for the main idea or feeling that the poet is trying to get across to you

Easier said than done. We have all read poems where our initial response is a kind of blank 'Ermmm . . .'. There are various ways round this problem. With the poems in *Songs of Innocence and of Experience*, for example, which go together as a group, you will begin to recognise certain words, simple ones such as 'joy' or 'weep', that come up again and again with a frequency that is more than accidental and that means that Blake is nudging you towards certain repeated themes. But more often we are faced with a lyric on its own, and that is when difficulty arises as we attempt to pin down the central idea or feeling that the poem is trying to convey. The way to deal with this difficulty is to interrogate your own responses.

What did the poem make you think of?
What did you feel as you read it?
What terms did the poet use to provoke those reactions in you?

If after asking yourself these questions and thinking about them carefully you are still drawing a blank, then remember above all the point I made in the first chapter about tensions, hopes and fears. Those are dominant moods of the Romantic period; you will not find them in every single lyric and you certainly will not find them expressed in exactly the same way in more than one, but most of the time the vital clue to the poem can be found if you try to isolate the *hope* it expresses; the *fear* it gives vent to; or the sense of *tension* between hope and fear, joy and sorrow, pain and pleasure, ideals and reality that we might find in it. When you have done this and think you have got hold of the main emotion or thought that the poem is setting up, then move on to the second step.

2   Read the poem again and see how the main idea or feeling is given precise shape by the choices and combinations of words that express it

We met the notion of choice and combination in Chapter 1, where I argued that it is the basis of any and every use of language, from the mumbled apology when you tread on someone's pet ferret in a bus queue to the pen-chewing, head-scratching business of writing a job application. Close scrutiny of the sorts of choices and combinations that go into the construction of a lyric poem are important for at least two reasons. First, the fact that it is a *poem* gives the writer more licence than if he or she were drawing up a train timetable or spelling out the fire regulations in a public building. It means that all the resources of language – alliteration, pun, symbol, rhyme, metaphor and so on – can be and indeed are used with a freedom and a flourish denied to the editor of timetables or the compiler of warning notices. And, secondly, the fact that it is a *lyric* means, as we have seen, that it is the place above all where poets go in order to be as precise and personal as they like, to convey with all the accuracy they can muster their own ideas or emotions. So look at those choices and combinations as closely as you can. Each one of them is like the movement of a sculptor, chiselling a bit here, sandpapering a fraction there, knocking off a lump in one place and rounding out a prominence in another, to give the completed object a specific shape and no other. A poem, like a statue, is a piece of raw material that has been worked on carefully to arrive at the particular dimensions and finish that it has in front of us. In the case of the poem, where the raw material is words, thinking about the choices and combinations and their implications that in the end constitute the work will help us to see the outline much more sharply. Once we have done that we can move on to the third step.

3 Focus closely on the two or three lines which were conclusive in fixing your sense of the poem's main idea or feeling

This third step is really only a refinement of the first two, a place where, by looking as minutely as you can at what for you was the core of the poem, you avoid the danger of vague impressions and even vaguer description of them. This core will be the line or lines where for you the poem's central idea or feeling, its tension, hope or fear, is most graphically and distinctively expressed. Here again, pay attention to the poet's particular choices and combinations of words and this will help you to see and to show why you have come away from the text with one set of responses rather than another.

4 Sum up your impressions of the poem as a whole

The fourth and final step is fairly self-explanatory. It is the moment when you look back at the ground you have covered in the first three steps and offer a summary description of it. Now is also the moment to mention other aspects of the poem which have not been part of your account so far but which you feel are worth highlighting because they made some contribution to the poem's effect, some addition to the distinctive way that reading it made you think or see. And now is also the time when you give a final shape to your response and so avoid leaving a messy jumble of impressions.

III

In order to get hold of this method properly it would obviously be helpful to see it at work as soon as possible, so let us now take one of the poems in Blake's *Songs of Innocence* and see what can be done with it using the method I have just outlined.

The poem I have chosen is the 'Nurse's Song':

When the voices of children are heard on the green
And laughing is heard on the hill,
My heart is at rest within my breast
And everything else is still.

'Then come home, my children, the sun is gone down
'And the dews of night arise;
'Come, come leave off play, and let us away
'Till the morning appears in the skies.'

'No, no, let us play, for it is yet day
'And we cannot go to sleep;
'Besides, in the sky the little birds fly
'And the hills are all cover'd with sheep.'

'Well, well, go & play till the light fades away
'And then go home to bed.'
The little ones leaped & shouted & laugh'd
And all the hills ecchoed.

I   Look for the main idea or feeling

If you run through the list of possibilities I suggested earlier (namely, tensions, hopes and fears) then it should be apparent after going through it a couple of times that this is primarily a poem of hope, hope that is conveyed through the laughter and delight of children. Even a glance through it at speed-reading pace would throw at you a whole series of simple words with pleasant and positive associations: *laughing*, *rest*, *still*, *home*, *sun*, *play*, *morning*, *sheep*, *light*, *bed*. Out of that selection the word that perhaps strikes a reader most is *play*, because it is repeated three times in a short lyric and because it is the issue around which the four sections of the poem are built. After an introductory stanza placing the children on the village green, they are told to 'leave off play' in the second stanza, contradict this with 'No, no, let us play' at the start of the third, and are given permission ('Well, well, go & play') at the start of the last. Just in case we miss it, Blake underlines the idea even further with an accompanying illumination at the bottom of the lyric showing a group of children, hands joined in a semicircle as the nurse sits and watches their game.

This much is clear from a couple of readings of 'Nurse's Song'. Our sense that the idea of the innocent play of children is important to Blake is reinforced as we proceed through other poems in *Songs of Innocence*. The illustrations to half-a-dozen of them ('The Ecchoing Green', 'The Blossom', 'The Chimney Sweeper', 'Laughing Song', 'The Divine Image' and 'Nurse's Song') depict groups of youngsters dancing, feasting or playing. The notion of innocence comes through in many ways, from major signposts such as the very title of the volume to minor details such as the repeated appearance of sheep, a common symbol of innocence in a Christian culture. There are sheep here in the third stanza of the 'Nurse's Song' and they feature in the illuminations to several more poems: to 'The Shepherd' and 'The Lamb' as we might expect, but also 'The Little Black Boy' and 'Spring'.

So far, so bland. To write hopeful poems about the innocent play of children scarcely strikes us now as very daring or original and suggests a potential career for Blake as a compiler of trite rhymes for birthday cards. But if we go back to the moment when 'Nurse's Song' was issued, to the social and historical context I described in the first chapter, then suddenly the poem reads differently. Blake was celebrating the right of children to play in the very generation when they were being herded off the village greens and into the new textile mills and mines in unprecedented numbers, forcing the historian E.P. Thompson to conclude about the period, 'the exploitation of little children, on this scale and with this intensity, was one of the most shameful events in our history' (*The Making of the English Working Class*, 1968, p. 384.)

Moreover, for Blake to emphasise the innocence of children in a volume issued in the summer of the French Revolution was not an innocent thing to do but an implicit challenge to what became a dominant and sharply contrasting view of children in the following years. Here, for example, is William Wilberforce, one of the leaders of the Evangelical revival in the Church of England, writing in *A Practical View of Chris-*

tianity in 1797: 'Remember we are all fallen creatures, born in sin and naturally depraved. Christianity recognises no innocence or goodness of heart.' Or listen to another Evangelical writer, Hannah More, whose tracts were distributed across Britain in their millions in the 1790s, writing in *Strictures on the Modern System of Female Education* in 1799. Children, she insists, have a 'corrupt nature and evil dispositions', adding that it is 'a fundamental error to consider children as innocent beings'. Bear those dreary remarks in mind, read 'Nurse's Song' again, and suddenly it is an exhilarating and defiant lyric. It sets itself against the harsh cries for discipline and repression issuing from those interests frightened by the French Revolution and fearful that it might cross the Channel.

2   Look at the choices and combinations of words that express the main idea or feeling

Now that we have isolated the main idea we can move on to thinking about the way Blake defines and colours it with the words he chooses. Perhaps the first thing to notice is how, every time that main idea is expressed, it is heavily underscored by a promptly following rhyming word: 'play . . . away' in line 7, 'play . . . day' in line 9, and 'play . . . away' again in line 13. If you doubt the impact of such a tiny device, you might reflect on the success with which advertisers, using exactly the same rhyming words, have in the past fixed a slogan in a lot of people's heads: 'A Mars a day helps you work, rest and play.' You must admit that the rhyme gives the line a punch that, say, 'A Mars a day helps you work, rest and get fat' somehow lacks.

And then we might note the extreme simplicity of the poem's vocabulary. Only about one word in every seven, for example, has more than one syllable, an extremely low proportion. (In that last sentence of mine, by contrast, nearly one word in two was polysyllabic.) This simple vocabulary is bolted together in the simplest possible way. Note, for instance, that nearly half of the lines (seven out of sixteen) begin with 'And', which, as a couple of minutes listening to the chatter of children would remind you, is much the easiest way to link statements together. Even though the speaker of most of the poem is the adult nurse, with the children replying to her in the third stanza, the language, and syntax of the poem is childlike, pitched at a level that the youngsters at whom Blake aimed the lyrics would find easy to understand. Certainly the changes Blake made to the 1784 version of the poem point in the direction of greater simplicity: in the 1789 vesion (printed above), the slightly fanciful 'tongues of children' in line 1 became the more explicit 'voices of children', while the polysyllable 'meadows' in line 12 was replaced by the easier-to-read monosyllable 'hills'. If Blake, as I argued in step 1, was trying to challenge some contemporary conceptions of childhood, then step 2 would suggest that he was trying to make sure the message would get through to children as well as adults.

3   Focus on the lines which clinch your sense of the poem's main idea or feeling

At this stage you need to avoid being anxious about your choice. Suppress the notion that a certain two or three lines represent the 'right' answer and to talk about any others would be wrong. There is no right or wrong answer here or in any other lyric, because the most significant lines will differ from reader to reader depending on her or his experiences and beliefs. All you can do is honestly consult you own responses to the lyric and pin down the moment in the poem where that response comes through most strikingly. So, for me, that moment in 'Nurse's Song' comes at the instant of tension in the poem, the second when all the general leaping and jollity is threatened. It is when the children contradict their nurse with that insistent, repeated negative in the third stanza: 'No, no, let us play, for it is yet day'. Think of common adult responses to the obstinacy of children at this point. 'Do as I say and get home before I give you a thick ear' might be one. In fact Blake himself describes just such a bitter response in the companion poem to this, the 'Nurse's Song' in *Songs of Experience*, where the children are silenced by the nurse's jealous insistence that their time is 'wasted in play'. But here in *Songs of Innocence*, after a laden pause before the fourth stanza, the nurse cheerfully concedes, 'Well, well, go & play till the light fades away'. Not only are the children disobedient, but, instead of getting eaten by a giraffe or catching pneumonia as punishment for their crime, their action is endorsed by an adult and they carry on enjoying themselves. By drawing his readers through this key moment of tension in the poem, Blake governs our response to his work and enables us to share some of the triumph of the children in the closing lines. You can get a firm grip on this or any lyric and the kind of effect it is striving to produce by searching for what seems to you to be its point of tension and thinking through the results of this tension and its resolution.

4 Sum up your impressions of the poem as a whole

Where has all that got us? We have seen that in sixteen very simply expressed lines Blake celebrates the innocent play of children. That play, as the accompanying illumination emphasises, is on a traditional village green without expensive equipment and with the children in a loose, harmonious group. Their shared pleasure is for a moment threatened by adult prohibition – and behind the nurse we can catch other contemporary voices, religious and economic, who were also determined to police children's lives. But here for once the youngsters win and the poem closes with their celebration of a small victory. Nature seems to signal her support for that celebration as 'all the hills ecchoed.' All of these things together – the laughing children, the relaxed adult, the echoing hills, the idyllic illumination – combine to convey Blake's own personal sense of delight in a scene shadowed by the way history was moving.

IV

Blake finished the *Songs of Innocence* in 1789. Looking back on those times Wordsworth later exulted in *The Prelude*,

Bliss was it in that dawn to be alive,
But to be young was very Heaven!
(1850 version, XI. 108–9)

The Americans had successfully concluded their War of Independence earlier in the decade, and in 1789, with the onset of the French Revolution, a new era of freedom seemed to be beginning in Europe. You can still catch the wonderful atmosphere of those times in the excited and optimistic lyrics of *Songs of Innocence*.

Blake issued the combined *Songs of Innocence and of Experience* in 1794. In the five years since *Songs of Innocence* everything, it seemed, had changed. Early in 1793 Britain and France had started a war that was to last on and off for a generation. At once support for the sort of radical ideas associated with the new France could be made to seem actively treacherous. The small circle of free spirits that had given Blake a sympathetic environment to work and speak in began to break up. In the fraught, hysterical climate of the war, the Government was able to drown opposing voices. Leading radicals such as the novelist Thomas

Holcroft and John Thelwall, friend of Wordsworth and Coleridge, were put on trial for treason (though happily Holcroft and Thelwall were acquitted). Blake's friend and fellow engraver William Sharp was also arrested for political reasons that year. Tom Paine had fled to France in 1792 shortly before being declared an outlaw. Mary Wollstonecraft, whose *Original Stories from Real Life* Blake had illustrated in 1791, moved to Paris in 1792 in search of a less repressive society. Things got even worse in 1795 with the so-called Gagging Acts, which made most forms of radical activity — meetings, demonstrations, organising, publishing — next to impossible. It was out of those sort of harsh experiences that Blake etched the *Songs of Experience*.

So the later poems belong to a different, more complicated world. We see this at the start of the new combined volume, whose full title is *Songs Of Innocence and Of Experience Shewing the Two Contrary States of the Human Soul*. The intriguing word here is 'contrary', a term Blake had used in a key passage of his visionary text called *The Marriage of Heaven and Hell*, which he worked on between 1790 and 1792: 'Without Contraries is no progression. Attraction and Repulsion, Reason and Energy, Love and Hate, are necessary to Human existence.' Those lines are worth pausing over because they take us into Blake's distinctive way of thinking. He sees the world as split between warring forces — 'Attraction and Repulsion, Reason and Energy, Love and Hate' — but he does not call for the triumph of one side and the suppression of the other. Rather, he sees the struggle between those forces as 'necessary to Human existence'. He does so because out of the contest of those contrary forces comes human advance, 'progression'.

And so it is too with those other contraries, innocence and experience. Innocence he sees as admirable and experience he notes is sometimes desolating, but he is not tempted on that basis to try to preserve innocence uncontaminated and resist experience as evil. Instead, these two 'Contrary States of the Human Soul' are seen, to borrow terms from *The Marriage of Heaven and Hell*, as 'necessary to Human existence'. Innocence without experience is on occasion naïve to the point of dangerous ignorance. It needs experience to grow to maturity. That experience can be brutal and appalling — think, for example, of the child chained and burned in 'A Little Boy Lost' is *Songs of Experience*. But to forbid experience in order to preserve innocence is no solution — look at the dismal chapel with '"Thou shalt not" writ over the door' in 'The Garden of Love' in *Songs of Experience* as an indictment of precisely that policy. The way forward seems to be an honest and innocent attempt to meet and go through experience, however terrifying, and thus learn to grow up. This I take to be the point of the pair of poems 'The Little Girl Lost' and 'The Little Girl Found' in *Songs of Experience*.

What I was trying to do in the last paragraph was put the combined *Songs of Innocence and of Experience* into an overall context in terms both of the history and experiences Blake was living through and the ideas he held at the time. Without that context the sharp change of tone from the laughing lyrics of *Innocence* to the anger of *Experience* can be puzzling and Blake's attitude to experience itself quite bewildering. However, the time has come to move away from wide generalisations and turn to a particular lyric, using the method outlined earlier in the chapter to open it up. The poem I have chosen from *Songs of Experience* is 'The Clod & the Pebble':

'Love seeketh not Itself to please,
'Nor for itself hath any care,
'But for another gives its ease,
'And builds a Heaven in Hell's despair.'

So sung a little Clod of Clay
Trodden with the cattle's feet,
But a Pebble of the brook
Warbled out these metres meet:

'Love seeketh only Self to please,
'To bind another to Its delight,
'Joys in another's loss of ease,
'And builds a Hell in Heaven's despite.'

I   Look for the main idea or feeling

The first time I read this poem I found it very frustrating. It seemed a muddle with no sense to it at all. In twelve lines we are given a view of love that is ascribed to a clod of clay; a pebble then expresses a more or less exactly opposite view; end of poem. Eventually I began to think that there must originally have been a fourth stanza, a stanza in which the poet stepped forward and presented his personal solution (it was supposed to be a lyric, after all), telling us who was right, the clod or the pebble, or more probably offering his own superior alternative to their muddy, stony conceptions. But no such luck. We are left in the air. Contrast the 'Nurse's Song' we looked at a few pages ago, where two opposite views were also stated ('Come, come, leave off play' against

'No, no, let us play') and a resolution was reached in the fourth stanza. Not here.

There is an easy but false response to this problem. It is in effect to supply that 'missing' fourth stanza, to guess at and tack on Blake's answer, but this ducks the question of why he chose not to supply it more obviously himself. After all, in poem after poem elsewhere in *Songs of Experience* Blake is blazingly clear about his position. So why not here?

The answer to that question I think is that here the tension cannot be resolved; the contraries are total. It is, precisely, a poem about unresolved tension. The clod's experience and belief lead it to define love in self-denying terms; the pebble's lead it to define love in selfish terms. Depending on who is doing the talking and where the speaker is speaking from, 'Love' means diametrically opposite things. That is what this lyric is about.

2   Look at the choices and combinations of words that express the main idea or feeling

Perhaps the most striking feature of the words used in this poem is the way they are symmetrically patterned in the first and last stanzas. Four of the six words in the first and ninth lines are the same. Apart from the reversal of 'Heaven' and 'Hell' and the shift from 'despair' to 'despite', the fourth and the twelfth lines are identical. It is as if Blake were determined to weight the scales equally, allowing exactly the same number of words (twenty-five) and more or less the same terms to both clod and pebble, so that the balance is not able to tip either way and remains poised, refusing to come down on one side or the other.

That sense of two opposite extremes, tensed against each other and refusing to compromise, is reinforced by the way the poem heaps up flatly contradictory terms. Run your eye through the text and you could pick up a series of pleasant vibrations: *Love, please, care, ease, Heaven, sung, delight, Joys*, and so on. Do the same thing again and you could come up with a completely contrary list: *despair, Clod, Trodden, bind, loss, Hell, despite*. Meanwhile the accompanying illumination declines to illuminate and remains idyllically and perversely unaware of the argument. It shows sheep and cattle bending down in perfect harmony to drink at the brook while, at the bottom of the page, a couple of frogs hop on the bank and a fatuous-looking duck drifts serenely past.

The last point to notice about the choices and combinations that make up the poem is the matter of the clod and the pebble themselves.

Why a clod and a pebble? Why not, say, a brick and a bucket, or Sid
and Serena? Asking those questions directs us to the middle stanza,
where the clod and pebble appear, so we need to look at that one more
closely.

3   Focus on the lines which clinch your sense of the poem's main idea or feeling

The poem's title draws the reader's attention to the clod and the pebble
and so nudges us towards the second stanza, where they are described
and where we can firm up our understanding of what the lyric is about:

> So sung a little Clod of Clay
> Trodden with the cattle's feet,
> But a Pebble of the brook
> Warbled out these metres meet:

We have a picture of the clay as 'little', trodden on and perhaps not very
bright – 'clod', meaning 'fool' as well as a lump of earth, was as common
a term in Blake's time as in ours. By contrast the pebble is in a much
easier environment, soothed by the soft water of the brook. Granted
that clay and pebbles cannot sing or warble, Blake is plainly using these
objects to stand for things other than themselves. Their description suggests on the one hand a view of love expressed by someone weak and
downtrodden, and on the other a view of love expressed by someone
tough and privileged. Hence it is possible, as some critics have conjec-
tured, that Blake is thinking here of traditional gender roles. The clay
offers a self-obliterating conception of love that exploited women have
been encouraged to accept, while the pebble's domineering notion of
love, based on binding another to its wishes, is a common feature of a
type of brute masculinity. Certainly the main point to grasp is that their
very different positions, trampled on the one hand and caressed on the
other, have produced in them a sharply contradictory set of values.

4   Sum up your impressions of the poem as a whole

Looking back at the last couple of pages, what comes strongly through
is the notion of tension, a tension between two positions that both poem
and illumination refuse to smooth out. We are given no middle way, no

compromise. What we have instead is precisely the sort of 'contrary' that Blake points to on the title-page of the collection, that clash between opposites which, as we have seen, Blake in *The Marriage of Heaven and Hell* regarded as necessary both to human existence and to human progress. If you think about the poem in this way, then I think you can see it as a typical lyric – a composition, in other words, in which the poet develops a personal view. Clashing, irreconcilable contraries were all around Blake in the 1790s, as hopes rose and were squashed, friends wrote intoxicating manifestos and then vanished into exile, men and women fought for a better world and then were checked and thrown back by reactionary forces. This lyric captures the essence of those times. It translates into its miniature, symbolic terms the massive confrontations of 'Hell' and 'Heaven', of liberation and repression, even of men and women and their roles, articulated by Blake's feminist friend Mary Wollstonecraft, and part of the very air that Blake breathed in London in those years. The poem arrives at no pat solution to those antagonisms any more than history itself did. It was a set of contradictions that, as Blake saw, would continue to be fought out for a long time, and he turns that political stalemate into the imaginative vision of this lyric.

#

I have tried to do a couple of things in this chapter. First, I have tried to give you an introductory sense of Blake the man and the history that surrounded him as he worked, so that you have some clues when you approach his lyrics and do not come to them 'cold'. Those clues are particularly necessary in Blake's case because, as we have seen, he does not float gently down the mainstream of English culture but cuts across it from a sharp angle, saying new and different things because of his new and different origins. Without some sense of that angle his lyrics can sometimes be confusing, for all their apparent simplicity. And, secondly, I have tried to offer a method for reading those lyrics more closely, so that you can move past second-hand ideas about the man and his age and begin to look at what, precisely and specifically, he does with those materials when he makes a poem. The most important thing now is for you to try out that method for yourself on other lyrics, and I hope that working slowly through two poems in this chapter, showing the method in practice, has given you the confidence to do that. The study of English literature is a mind-rottingly dull business as long as all it involves is reproducing the opinions of critics, lecturers and teachers. But, once you take hold of a method or a theory that you can use to produce your own insights and analyses, then it can become an intensely exciting subject – educational in the literal sense, because it draws out of you ideas you did not know you had, and educational in the best sense because it allows you to think freely for yourself.

Two suggestions, then, before you apply that method to other lyrics in *Songs of Innocence and of Experience*. In this chapter I have looked at poems on their own because that is the obvious way to start. But their titles will tell you that some poems clearly go together: for example, we examined the 'Nurse's Song' in *Songs of Innocence*, but there is also one in *Songs of Experience*. Once you have worked carefully at individual poems as we have in this chapter, then the next step is to move on to the paired or contrary lyric, and then out from there to others. Each lyric, remember, expresses a mood, a moment, a fleeting feeling. By connecting those up from different lyrics, you begin to build a picture of Blake's value system, the ideas and beliefs as a whole that structure *Songs of Innocence and of Experience* and its individual parts.

The second suggestion is that you should try at some stage to consult an edition that reproduces the illuminations that Blake etched with each lyric. Printing costs inevitably mean that the editions most people can afford to buy will not include these and, although it is quite possible to work with the poems on their own, it is a touch lopsided to study one half of Blake's creation and not the other. I am not insisting that you have to become an art historian as well as a literary critic. It is simply that Blake's illuminations can sometimes, unsurprisingly, illuminate – can, in other words, help you towards a sense of what a poem is trying to say. Reading Blake can be difficult enough without ignoring some of the signals he supplies. Your college or local library should have an edition that reproduces the illuminations along with the poems, and there is also a reasonably priced paperback published by Oxford University Press and edited by Geoffrey Keynes which has them too.

This is perhaps the most important chapter in this book because in it I have tried to offer a method for reading a lyric that will apply not just to Blake's poems but also to the lyrics of Wordsworth, Coleridge, Keats, Hands and Robinson that you will come across in your studies and that we shall be looking at in the following chapters. Here I have spelt that method out and shown two examples of it at work, so in subsequent chapters I shall take it as read and apply it without much rehearsal.

Remember all the time that the method is designed to do two main things: first, to provide the tools so that you can work freely on your own and are not condemned to reproduce the opinions of others; and, second, to help you focus your study of a lyric on its main idea or feeling, giving you in the end a clear view of the poem as a whole rather than a jumble of impressions.

3

READING WORDSWORTH'S SHORTER POEMS: *LYRICAL BALLADS*

I

IN 1798 a slim volume containing less than two dozen poems was published anonymously. The title page said simply *Lyrical Ballads, with a Few Other Poems*. The authors we now know were Wordsworth and Coleridge, then young and relatively unknown poets. The fact that only five hundred copies were printed indicates that the publisher expected only average sales, but over the years the reputation and significance of this book grew to the point where it became one of the best-remembered landmarks in English literary history. Gathering my thoughts when I set about writing this chapter, I came across a series of claims by various writers that testify to this status. 'The real starting point of Romantic poetry', said one critic. 'A major event in our literature and culture', added another. 'The most important volume of verse in English since the Renaissance, for it began modern poetry', asserted a third.

We need to be aware of these evaluations when we approach *Lyrical Ballads*, but also a little cautious about them. To date Romantic literature from 1798 was in part a way of excluding from literary history that awkward, independent, radical poet Blake, which is one reason why I started this book with him. It also diverted attention from prose writers such as Tom Paine, Mary Wollstonecraft and William Godwin and poets like Elizabeth Hands and Mary Robinson, who were widely read and crucially influential in the early 1790s and who asked challenging questions that later literary critics sometimes preferred to ignore.

However, the fact that *Lyrical Ballads* has been put to this use is no fault of Wordsworth and Coleridge.or of their poetry, and it is certainly true that we can trace important departures in English poetry back to the poems of *Lyrical Ballads* and their constituents. To be specific about those constituents we need to look at the poems more closely, and I should like to do that in a moment, using the method outlined in the last chapter. But first a potential problem needs clearing away. It concerns the very title, *Lyrical Ballads*. At first sight this can be a bit puzzling, rather as if Wordsworth and Coleridge had called their volume *Short Long Verses*. After all, the lyric, as we have seen, is usually a brief poem that conveys a moment of intense feeling and the author's personal reading of it. A ballad, by contrast, is a traditional form of narrative poetry whose most obvious element is the telling of a story, often involving a disaster which has nothing to do with the poet personally.

We can get round this problem if we look at the Advertisement that Wordsworth wrote for the volume and that was set out on its opening pages. 'The majority of the following poems are to be considered as experiments', he insists in the third sentence of that Advertisement. The experiments are designed to break away from 'the gaudiness and inane phraseology of many modern writers' and to use instead the language of 'the middle and lower classes of society'. If you imagine Wordsworth and Coleridge setting out in that direction, then I think you can see why they would very soon turn to the ballad, because there above all is the most obvious example of a vigorous, unpretentious form that uses popular language for poetic purposes. It is the very place to go, in short, if you are sick of 'gaudiness and inane phraseology'. As most critics note, very few poems in *Lyrical Ballads* are ballads in the sense I have just described; but, if 'ballad' is defined in the loose sense of a poem in very simple language that pays sympathetic attention to human sufferings, we can see its spirit as a constant presence in Wordsworth and Coleridge's volume.

II

At this point, let us look at one of the *Lyrical Ballads* using the method for the lyric described in Chapter 2. I have chosen 'Lines Written in Early Spring':

I heard a thousand blended notes,
While in a grove I sate reclined,
In that sweet mood when pleasant thoughts
Bring sad thoughts to the mind.

To her fair works did Nature link   5
The human soul that through me ran;
And much it grieved my heart to think
What man has made of man.

Through primrose tufts, in that green bower,
The periwinkle trailed its wreaths;   10
And 'tis my faith that every flower
Enjoys the air it breathes.

The birds around me hopped and played,
Their thoughts I cannot measure: –
But the least motion which they made,   15
It seemed a thrill of pleasure.

The budding twigs spread out their fan,
To catch the breezy air;
And I must think, do all I can,
That there was pleasure there.   20

If this belief from heaven be sent,
If such be Nature's holy plan,
Have I not reason to lament
What man has made of man?

I Look for the main idea or feeling

I chose this lyric because it is one that, as a student, I quite liked but
found difficulty in saying very much about. I had been told that
Wordsworth had a deep love of nature and that seemed obvious enough
from the text, but once you had said that about it you tended to dry
up, which still left you with about four pages and fifty-three minutes
to fill before they let you out. Is there anything else worth saying about
these two dozen lines, and how do you find it?

Well, if we take up the notion of tensions, hopes and fears that we
used in the earlier chapters, we can I think see that there is a revealing
and curious tension that persists through the piece. The speaker in the
very first stanza describes himself as being

> In that sweet mood when pleasant thoughts
> Bring sad thoughts to the mind

which is an odd thing to say, because for most people most of the time a 'sweet mood' and 'pleasant thoughts' are not normally linked at once to their opposite, 'sad thoughts'.

But this opposition runs right through the poem. The speaker is 'grieved' in the second stanza and claims he has 'reason to lament' in the last one. And yet at the same time the lyric is packed with delight, as you can see if you run your eye quickly down the page: *fair*, *sweet*, *enjoys*, *played*, *pleasure*, and so on. The pleasure in the poem seems to be associated with what are called in the second stanza the 'fair works' of Nature which the poem lists: the flowers in stanza three, the birds which are the subject of stanza four, and the budding twigs in stanza five. But cutting across this is a sorrow associated with man, a grief that inter-rupts the pleasure whenever the speaker thinks of 'What man has made of man'. He uses that phrase in the second stanza and repeats it to underscore it in the very last line of the poem. So the text seems to work with a simple, unresolved tension between, on the one hand, natural objects which are a source of pleasure and, on the other, man and his works which inspire grief.

2 Look at the choices and combinations of words that express the main idea or feeling

This simple tension begins to get a bit more complicated if we look closely at the exact way the speaker expresses it. For example, where is he? He tells us he is sitting in 'a grove' in the second line, a place he refers to later as a 'green bower'. If you look up 'grove' and 'bower' in a dictionary, you will get a picture of a shady retreat created by careful planning, planted round with trees and often with vegetation trained on some kind of lattice work. It will also help you to know that Wordsworth wrote the poem in the spring of 1798 in the grounds of Alfoxden, a substantial house in Somerset where he was living at the time. So what we visualise is not nature in some raw, untamed state, which might have been the case had Wordsworth written, say, 'forest' or 'swamp', but instead a cultivated landscape, nature as produced and reproduced by generations of human labour – in short, the garden scenery of southern England.

This sense of nature and man in productive harmony is further reinforced if we look at the way the speaker describes natural objects. Again and again he humanises them. Nature, for a start, is given a gender and is called 'her' in line 5. Her works are given human attributes and human emotions: we are told in stanza three that flowers breathe and enjoy doing so; in stanza four, that birds hop and play and think; and, in stanza five, that twigs have a fan which they use to catch the breeze. All of these things, in other words, seem to function in recognisably human ways rather than in some mysterious animal or vegetable way. Indeed, it is the perception of a shared life process that provides the 'link' between the human soul and nature's works that is the speaker's starting point in the second stanza.

So the poem is not working with some sort of crude contrast between rotten people and lovable trees – or, if it is, the poet is choosing terms that make the contrast impossible to sustain, because when he describes those trees, flowers and birds and the pleasures they give him he does so in terms that irresistibly remind us of human beings. Man, it seems, both depresses the poet when he thinks about what man has made of man and yet delights him when he relaxes in a man-made landscape and watches birds and flowers acting in ways that remind him of simple human pleasures such as playing and breathing. There is plainly a contradiction here which the poet is wrestling to resolve, and indeed evidence of that struggle disrupts the text as the poem moves towards its conclusion: 'I must think, do all I can'.

3 Focus on the lines which clinch your sense of the poem's main idea or feeling

Let us look at the last stanza, which is where we might expect the contradiction to come closest to a resolution. The first thing that strikes me about this stanza is that the language is religious: *belief, heaven, holy*. A vague divine authority, referred to as 'heaven' in line 21 and 'Nature' in line 22, has, it seems, organised the world in such a way that the 'pleasant thoughts' and pleasurable activities which the poem has depicted are possible, but lamentation comes when the speaker stops to think what human beings have done with these possibilities. In twenty-four lines the poet does not have space to be precise about who this divinity actually is or what human failings he is thinking of, so inevitably readers will fill those spaces with their own beliefs and experiences.

It is worth nothing that Wordsworth himself filled the space differently as time passed. As originally published (1798), the last stanza of the poem read,

> If I these thoughts may not prevent,
> If such be of my creed the plan,
> Have I not reason to lament
> What man has made of man?

This became, in all editions of Wordsworth's poetry published after 1815,

> If this belief from heaven be sent,
> If such be Nature's holy plan,
> Have I not reason to lament
> What man has made of man?

The later version introduces 'heaven' and 'Nature' as authorities for the beliefs that the poem describes, whereas in the original version the ideas had simply been thoughts bubbling up in Wordsworth's own mind to form 'my creed'. In short, the later, more orthodoxly Christian Wordsworth interprets the experience in religious terms, mourning man's wrecking of the 'holy plan'. But the earlier Wordsworth responded to the experience in a slightly but significantly different way, being simultaneously moved and depressed by his own belief in the simple beauties of life and by his sense of despair at the course of human history.

4   Sum up your impressions of the poem as a whole

'Lines Written in Early Spring' is, on the surface, a plain-enough poem that bears out the Advertisement's rejection of 'gaudiness and inane phraseology'. The language is as straightforward as in the Blake lyrics we looked at in the last chapter. Much of it is monosyllabic and everyday, and, apart from *periwinkle*, which the context would tell you is a flower, the longest words in the poem (*lament*, *reclined*, and so on) are unlikely to have you reaching for a dictionary.

The meaning these words convey is at first sight plain enough too. The speaker's joy in the 'fair works' of nature is contrasted with his 'sad thoughts' when he remembers 'What man has made of man'. That contrast seems to be clinched when we look at the final stanza, where the situation the poem has described is explained in a conventionally religious way: a 'holy plan' on the one hand, and human failure on the other. This sharp focus begins to blur when we notice, first, that the speaker represents nature in human terms and takes delight in its human qualities, and, second, that the religious reading of the experience in the final stanza, which seems to clarify the lyric's meaning, was not part of Wordsworth's original and more ambiguous interpretation. The poem expresses both enchantment with human capacities and grief about human behaviour. Quite how they are related is not finally clear; and indeed Wordsworth himself was unclear about their relations and so changed the ending in order to clarify them.

III

I think that that is as far as a close reading of this lyric can take us. To try to go any further is to be tempted into all sorts of absurd ingenuities, as words get wrung bone dry in a search for meanings that they cannot feasibly hold, and phrases set off speculative jaunts that end up quite out of sight of the main thrust of the poem. We have seen that 'Lines Written in Early Spring' is a typical *Lyrical Ballad* in that it raises fundamental questions about human beings and their natural environment and the relation between the two, questions that are at the centre of much of Wordsworth's best work. But we now need to move out from these twenty-four lines and into Wordsworth's life if we are to get the fuller answers that will allow us to go back to the poem with enhanced understanding.

Whenever I try to arrive at an accurate picture of Wordsworth the man, I am struck by the way that you can use the evidence to produce two almost entirely different portraits. First, you can construct a standard late-eighteenth-century gentleman of leisure. He was born in 1770 and brought up in the largest house in Cockermouth, Cumberland, where his father was business and law agent to Sir James Lowther, later Lord Lonsdale, one of the biggest landowners in the county. In addition Wordsworth's family had some private income from a couple of small estates that enabled them to keep a pair of servants. They also had enough comfortably-off relatives to enable Wordsworth, although both his parents were dead before he was fourteen, to afford to move on from Hawkshead Grammar School to St John's College, Cambridge, in 1787. After Cambridge he toyed with the idea of becoming a French tutor, but the extraordinary generosity of friends and acquaintances meant that he never had to work systematically for a living outside writing poetry. From September 1795 to June 1797, for example, John Pinney allowed Wordsworth and his sister Dorothy to live rent-free at Racedown Lodge, Dorset. Earlier, in January 1795, Raisley Calvert left Wordsworth and Dorothy a legacy of £900. That sum might sound modest nowadays, but its purchasing power then can be gauged from the fact that a farmworker's wages were about 40p a week and a doctor's income less than £300 a year.

And yet alongside that picture of apparent privilege you can draw a second and very different portrait of Wordsworth. When his father died in 1783 it emerged that he had been paid little or nothing over the years by Lord Lonsdale, and the family were forced into a long and wearying legal battle for the money they were owed. Payment was not finally secured until 1802, by which time Wordsworth had learned a healthy disrespect for rank and wealth. The family loans that financed his education and needed repaying, delays in receiving the Calvert legacy, and his own generous habit of promptly loaning cash to help friends out of trouble meant that William and Dorothy were by no means rich at this time; for instance, Dorothy estimated that the pair of them lived off £110 in the year from the summer of 1797 to the summer of 1798.

Above all, this second, radical Wordsworth went to France and spent more than a year – from November 1791 to December 1792 – in a society pulling itself apart and remaking itself in ways at once exhilarating and terrifying. In July 1789 the working people of Paris had started the French Revolution by storming the Bastille, the prison that represented all the brute tyranny of the old regime, and three months later they marched out to King Louis XVI's palace at Versailles and brought him back to Paris a virtual prisoner. The slogan by which the French Revolution is still popularly remembered ('Liberty, Equality, Fraternity') can even now brush past cynicism to touch us with the excitement of a time when men and women broke out of all the dreary maxims and shabby privations that had crushed their lives for generations and set about building a society that met rather than repressed human needs and desires. Looking back later in *The Prelude*, the long narrative poem in which he examines his own development as a poet, at a time when his politics were very different, Wordsworth was honest enough to recapture and pay tribute to the liberating delights of those days:

> Bliss was it in that dawn to be alive,
> But to be young was very Heaven! O times,
> In which the meagre, stale, forbidding ways
> Of custom, law, and statute, took at once
> The attraction of a country in romance!
> (1850 version, XI. 108–12)

In revolutionary France, where he had gone with vague plans to polish up his French so as to become a language tutor, Wordsworth met a surgeon's daughter, Annette Vallon, and fell in love for the first time in his life. Their child Caroline was born in December 1792. Also in France, Wordsworth got to know Michel Beaupuy, a soldier in the army of the revolutionary republic. In four months of intense friendship, Wordsworth learned from Beaupuy more politics than most people learn in a lifetime, and it was politics not as abstract theory but as day-to-day struggle. Wordsworth memorably records a typical instance of that education in *The Prelude*:

> And when we chanced
> One day to meet a hunger-bitten girl,
> Who crept along fitting her languid gait
> Unto a heifer's motion, by a cord
> Tied to her arm, and picking thus from the lane
> Its sustenance, while the girl with pallid hands
> Was busy knitting in a heartless mood
> Of solitude, and at the sight my friend
> In agitation said, ''Tis against *that*
> That we are fighting', I with him believed
> That a benignant spirit was abroad
> Which might not be withstood, that poverty
> Abject as this would in a little time
> Be found no more. . . .
> (1850 version, IX. 509–22)

Wordsworth was in Paris in October 1792 shortly after the September massacres, the moment when the Revolution began to turn sour for some observers as the Jacobins, the party of the lower middle class and the artisans, turned on the upper middle class Girondins in a fight for power. But, contrary to some suggestions, Wordsworth was not at

once disillusioned and did not promptly turn into a Tory. Back in
England in 1793 he was still prepared to defend revolutionary violence.
This is plain in his reply to the Bishop of Llandaff, who had published
a reactionary sermon entitled 'The Wisdom and Goodness of God
having made both Rich and Poor'. Wordsworth wrote:

> You say: 'I fly with terror and abhorrence even from the altar of Liberty,
> when I see it stained with the blood of the aged, of the innocent, of the
> defenceless sex, of the ministers of religion, and of the faithful adherents
> of a fallen monarch.' What! have you so little knowledge of the nature of
> man as to be ignorant that a time of revolution is not the season of true
> Liberty? Alas, the obstinacy and perversion of man is such that she is too
> often obliged to borrow the very arms of Despotism to overthrow him,
> and, in order to reign in peace, must establish herself by violence. She
> deplores such stern necessity, but the safety of the people, her supreme
> law, is her consolation.

What I have been driving at for the past few pages is the idea that
there are at least two sides to Wordsworth. On the one hand there is
the respectable gentleman – lawyer's son, Cambridge-educated, living on various incomes, bequests and properties, the kind of man who
later slipped easily into Government sinecures, as witness his appoint-
ment as Distributor of Stamps for Westmorland in 1813 and as Poet
Laureate in 1843. But inside that Wordsworth is another Wordsworth,
embittered by the way his father's labour was exploited by an aristocrat, jolted by the premature death of his parents, and then emotion-
ally, sexually and politically amazed by the French Revolution. For a few
glowing years in the 1790s and beyond, those two Wordsworths worked
in creative tension to produce some of the best-known poems in English
literature before respectability triumphed.

It will help you to understand the style and the content of *Lyrical
Ballads* if you hold on to this picture of Wordsworth as a passionate man
briefly but radically at odds with the tastes and the values of the British
establishment, into which he was born and into which he was eventually absorbed. Think of him as the young poet whose odd lifestyle so
upset neighbours around Alfoxden, where he lived and wrote most of
the poems in *Lyrical Ballads* between July 1797 and June 1798, that
Government spies reported on him and Coleridge as possible French
agents and his landlady refused to renew his lease. Think of those things
and you begin to see *Lyrical Ballads* freshly illuminated. You can detect
how some of the angry politics of the reply to the Bishop of Llandaff
are still there and are being thought through into literary terms. At a

time when British culture was dominated by the mood of reaction that had begun to set in as early as 1793, when war against revolutionary France had started, Wordsworth insists against that mood in the Preface to the 1800 edition of *Lyrical Ballads* that in the poems he will choose incidents and subjects from 'low and rustic life'. The choice is made because in that condition 'the essential passions of the heart find a better soil in which they can attain their maturity' and are 'less under restraint'. And he goes on to affirm that he will adopt 'the very language too of these men' because 'from their rank in society . . . being less under the influence of social vanity they convey their feelings and emotions in simple and unelaborated expressions'.

It is not just hindsight that deciphers the politics of Wordsworth's enterprise in *Lyrical Ballads*. It was seen clearly enough by contemporaries, and even such a supporter of Whig proposals for reform as Francis Jeffrey, writing in the *Edinburgh Review* in October 1802, was keen to throttle the radical principles underlying *Lyrical Ballads*:

> But the mischief of this new system is not confined to the depravation of language only: it extends to the sentiments and emotions, and leads to the debasement of all those feelings which poetry is designed to communicate. It is absurd to suppose that an author should make use of the language of the vulgar to express the sentiments of the refined. . . . The love, or grief, or indignation of an enlightened and refined character is not only expressed in a different language but is in itself a different emotion from the love, or grief, or anger of a clown, a tradesman, or a market-wench.

It is not literature that is being talked about here. The terms that carry value –*mischief, depravation, debasement, vulgar, refined, enlightened, market-wench* – amount to a *class* condemnation of Wordsworth's practice.

Wordsworth later moved away from his youthful radicalism, and in many ways, as we shall see in the next chapter, *The Prelude* is an account of and an attempt to justify that movement. The money flowing from the settlement of Lord Lonsdale's debt in 1802 and the gift in 1803 of a small estate at Applethwaite by a Tory admirer, Sir George Beaumont, are just two of the stages in that process. Wordsworth was shifted towards a place in society which distanced him from his youthful radicalism, a period in his life which supplied energies on which he continued to draw for a while but no longer values by which he was prepared to live.

But *Lyrical Ballads* remains as the triumphant product of those radical energies. The collection opens, as we have seen, with the 1798 Advertisement, which draws attention to and boldly defends the use of plain language in the poems. This defence switches into an attack, in the 1800 Preface, on the eighteenth-century standards of elegance and decorum which had produced the 'gaudiness and inane phraseology' that Wordsworth rejects. Instead he aims at 'a selection of language really used by men'. And this plain language will be used to describe what he calls 'incidents and situations from common life'. Try to imagine for a moment the scandal of that enterprise in a society whose politics and taste were still substantially dominated by the sort of stout, reactionary gentry you might have encountered in Jane Austen's novels.

And then, when you turn to the poems themselves, you find that again and again it is the powerless and dispossessed who are at the centre of those texts. It is their experiences that are celebrated, their sorrows that are recorded, their cause that is championed in their contacts with the powerful. Indeed, it is that celebrating, recording and championing that explains how many of the poems, which at first sight may seem to be about trivial matters, came to be written in the first place. Look, for examples of what I mean, at 'The Female Vagrant' or 'Goody Blake and Harry Gill', at 'Simon Lee' or 'The Idiot Boy', at 'We are Seven' or 'Anecdote for Fathers'. Every time it is the authority figure – parent, say, or landowner – who is in the wrong, and the outcast or the child who is right.

The implicit politics of this poetry is made explicit in the letter Wordsworth sent in June 1801 along with a copy of *Lyrical Ballads* to Charles James Fox, the leader of the Whig Opposition in the House of Commons. Wordsworth wrote,

> But recently by the spreading of manufactures through every part of the country, by the heavy taxes upon postage, by workhouses, Houses of Industry, and the invention of Soup-shops, &c. &c. superadded to the encreasing disproportion between the price of labour and that of the necessities of life, the bonds of domestic feeling among the poor . . . have been weakened, and in innumerable instances entirely destroyed.

In the light of this letter it becomes clear that what Wordsworth is doing in the poems is at once capturing and protesting against that weakening and destruction as it sliced up the lives of the individuals in, say, 'The Old Cumberland Beggar' or 'Michael'. You can thus read these poems as a brave attempt to educate the way readers felt, to put them back in touch with emotions and with people that were being uprooted and discarded.

Lyrical Ballads can then start to come alive as the poems of a man who liked ordinary people and simple pleasures but who was angry at what 'man has made of man'. That is what 'Lines Written in Early Spring' is all about. He wanted to push the desires and distresses of the rural poor right into the centre of national awareness. Read the poems in *Lyrical Ballads* in that spirit and they can still release a lot of the power that is stored in them from Wordsworth's life and his contact with the idealism of the French Revolution. I find that they begin to work in ways that they do not if you approach them simply as nature poetry. The reverence I was encouraged to pay to nature poetry at school never emerged for me; I thought it had some of the sanctimonious air of compulsory church-going, or it reminded me of regimented walks on dreary February afternoons looking for signs of spring. But if you think of those poems as being primarily about the needs and the pleasures of ordinary life and ordinary people in a world bent on suppressing those things, then they can still stir us in important and life-enhancing ways.

IV

All of that may be true, but we still have to come back to the fact that most people know Wordsworth as a nature poet whose major poem *The Prelude* is substantially about his recollections of encounters with nature in various forms. Poetry, Wordsworth claimed in the Preface to *Lyrical Ballads*, 'takes its origin from emotion recollected in tranquillity', and it is the recollection of the emotions inspired by nature that provided Wordsworth with the subject matter for a lot of his poetry. But before we move on to *The Prelude* we need to bring these notions of 'recollection' and 'nature' a little more sharply into focus. We need to understand how, for Wordsworth, the process of recollection actually works and we need to understand what this vague word 'nature' really means. Stephen Prickett, in an essay in the book he edited called *The Romantics* (London, 1981), traces nine different shades of meaning for the term 'nature' available in the Romantic period. It will obviously help prevent a lot of possible confusion if we try to sort out what the term meant in practice for Wordsworth before we go much further. The best and most convenient place to start doing that is the long meditative lyric 'Lines written a Few Miles above Tintern Abbey', which Wordsworth placed as the last poem in *Lyrical Ballads*.

At 160 lines, 'Tintern Abbey' is five to ten times as long as the other lyrics we have looked at closely so far in this book (and so too long to quote here in full), but the same method of analysis we have employed before will work again here and is indeed essential if we are to avoid getting lost. So let us apply it. (The edition of *Lyrical Ballads* I shall use is that edited by R.L. Brett and A.R. Jones and published in 1963.)

I   Look for the main idea or feeling

If we start, as we did with the earlier examples, by looking for the sources of tension, hope and fear in the poem, then we come up at once with two sources of hope. First, there is the scenery round the River Wye, those 'forms of beauty' (l. 24) whose memory over the years has brought Wordsworth 'sensations sweet' (l. 28). Secondly, in the last third of the poem, there is Wordsworth's sister Dorothy, 'my dearest Friend' (l. 116), and the pleasure he derives from sharing with her these scenes and the delight they provide. If we now move on to look for the negative feelings and fears that these 'sensations sweet' are tensed against, we meet roughly the same structure of emotion that we found in 'Lines Written in Early Spring'. What seem to depress the poet are the various aspects of urban life he notes – 'the din/Of towns and cities' (ll. 26–7) with their 'fretful stir' (l. 53) – and the experiences he has there, whether 'rash judgments' and 'the sneers of selfish men' (l. 130) or simply 'the dreary intercourse of daily life' (l. 132). So, as in 'Lines Written in Early Spring', nature appears to provide the speaker with warm memories which are both sadly contrasted with and in some ways compensate for the grief which flows from other human beings and what they have made of the world.

2   Look at the choices and combinations of words that express the main idea or feeling

As I noted earlier, we need to be a bit more specific about both nature and the processes of memory or recollection if we are to do more than reproduce the weariest platitudes of Wordsworth criticism, so let us see exactly how these ideas get expressed in 'Tintern Abbey'. Right from the start of the poem, emphasis is placed on the remoteness of the natural scenery in which the poet rejoices:

> Once again
> Do I behold those steep and lofty cliffs,
> Which on a wild secluded scene impress
> Thoughts of more deep seclusion . . .
>
> (ll. 4–7)

'Steep and lofty cliffs' and 'wild' suggest a deserted spot, and, just in case we do not realise that, the repetition in 'secluded . . . seclusion' makes it unavoidable. If there are a few people about, they are no more than hermits in what are essentially 'houseless woods' (l. 21), and it is this landscape that brings Wordsworth consolation in 'towns and cities' (l. 27). So the first meaning of nature that emerges from the poem is simply the countryside as opposed to the town – and, more particularly, wild and secluded countryside more or less empty of inhabitants.

If we look for the reasons why this nature has such capacity to soothe the poet, then we shall begin to see the second sense in which the word is used in the poem. In nature there seems to be 'A presence that disturbs me with the joy/Of elevated thoughts' (ll. 95–6)), 'a spirit, that impels/All thinking things' (ll. 101–2). Nature is

> The anchor of my purest thoughts, the nurse
> The guide, the guardian of my heart, and soul
> Of all my moral being.
>
> (ll. 110–12)

'Nature' gets a capital letter for the first time in line 123 and supplies Wordsworth and his sister with their 'chearful faith that all which we behold/Is full of blessings' (ll. 134–5). As the poem moves to its conclusion, Wordsworth describes himself as a 'worshipper of Nature' (l. 153).

As we run back through these terms, we can note that nature is no longer just landscape – trees and grass and cliffs – but an active force, a 'presence' and 'a spirit', with immense power. It is a power that is wholly positive, inspiring and anchoring the poet's most pure and elevated thoughts and acting as a moral guide and guardian. Nature, in fact, seems to be some sort of goddess – hence the capital letter and the reference to 'her' in line 124 – clothed in heavily religious terminology: *sublime, spirit, soul, moral, prayer, faith, blessings, service, worshipper, holier* are just some of the words associated with Nature in the last half of the poem. In short, the goddess Nature, manifesting herself in and through wild, secluded countryside, occupies in 'Tintern Abbey' the place usually filled by the Christian God in the dominant culture. This religious conception of Nature is matched by the language of the poem as a whole, which is altogether more dense and elevated than the deliberately simple expression of most of the other poems in *Lyrical Ballads*. Look, for example, at the two long, winding and complexly qualified sentences that run from line 94 to line 112 and compare them with the six brief, symmetrical statements that make up the twenty-four lines of 'Lines Written in Early Spring'.

I remember reading 'Tintern Abbey' for the first time as a teenager and being sceptical about this quasi-divine nurse, guide and guardian. I went out, anticipating elevated thoughts, and stood waiting in front of an oak tree. There was a dead rabbit at the bottom of it. Not a lot happened and then it started raining. I went home and, deciding that either Wordsworth was a twit or I was a philistine, wondered anxiously if I could avoid writing about him in the exam. Going back to the poem now, I can understand why all I saw that day was rain and a rotting rabbit. Look at these lines:

> Therefore am I still
> A lover of the meadows and the woods,
> And mountains; and of all that we behold
> From this green earth; of all the mighty world
> Of eye and ear, both what they half-create,
> And what perceive. . . .
>
> (ll. 103–8)

The key notion here is 'half-create'. For Wordsworth, we do not simply 'perceive' the world around us in some passive way; we actually work on those perceptions to create something else. I was waiting for the rain and the oak and the rabbit to do something by themselves, and of course nothing happened. But, in Wordsworth's view, what memory does is take hold of these perceptions and operate on them to produce the 'sensations sweet' that fill the poem. So memory is not some sort of computer that numbly records any data you care to put into it and then pumps it straight back out again on request. It is rather an ability we have to seize on a selection of sights, impressions and sounds and actively arrange them into new patterns with new meanings. For example, right at the start of the poem Wordsworth claims that 'I . . . connect/The landscape with the quiet of the sky' (ll. 5–8). It is through these connections that he forges in imagination that the 'dizzy raptures' (l. 86) come. What Wordsworth is actually looking at is not my damp oak or his section of the Wye valley but rather what he calls in line 62 'the picture of the mind' – something, in other words, drawn in his own head from the sensations he receives rather than a mere print-out of those sensations.

To take this point a stage further: the notes on 'Tintern Abbey' in most Wordsworth editions will tell you that the version of the Wye valley we get in this poem is historically not very accurate. The first thirty lines give us a picture of 'a wild secluded scene' and 'houseless woods' with little more than the odd vagrant about. In fact, as Mary Moorman remarks in her biography of Wordsworth, the river at that time would have been full of shipping, transporting timber and coal from the Forest of Dean. The 'wreathes of smoke' that Wordsworth guesses might originate from 'some hermit's cave' almost certainly came from the furnaces of one of the several charcoal manufacturers on the river bank. In one sense this does not matter: this is, after all, a meditative lyric rather than a monograph on industry in late-eighteenth-century Monmouthshire and Gloucestershire. But for our understanding of Wordsworth it is crucial. It reveals that for him memory is not an inert register but rather a powerful capacity that works hand in hand with imagination and ideology to fabricate the images and ideas that he needs in order to survive the 'din/Of towns and cities' (ll. 26–7) and 'the fever of the world' (l. 54).

3 Focus on the lines which clinch your sense of the poem's main idea or feeling

The reading of 'Tintern Abbey' which I have just offered is summed up for me in a single sentence, towards the end of the lyric, where Wordsworth applies the experience he has already described at length in himself to his sister Dorothy:

> Therefore let the moon
> Shine on thee in thy solitary walk;
> And let the misty mountain winds be free
> To blow against thee: and in after years,
> When these wild ecstasies shall be matured
> Into a sober pleasure, when thy mind
> Shall be a mansion for all lovely forms,
> Thy memory be as a dwelling-place
> For all sweet sounds and harmonies; Oh! then,
> If solitude, or fear, or pain, or grief,
> Should be thy portion, with what healing thoughts
> Of tender joy wilt thou remember me,
> And these my exhortations!
>
> (ll. 135–47)

First, there are the encounters with secluded nature: the 'solitary walk' where the mind selects and connects impressions – 'the moon' with 'the misty mountain winds', for example. Then years later memory takes hold of these impressions. They will not, Wordsworth expects, mature of their own accord; rather, they 'shall be matured/Into a sober plea- sure' in the 'mansion', the 'dwelling-place', of the mind – terms which reinforce the notion of memory as a faculty that constructs rather than passively records. Maturing and constructing in this way, memory can thus half-create and release Nature's semi-divine powers, the 'healing thoughts' and 'tender joy' which are pitched against the sorrows of life. Yet at the same time those sorrows disrupt the passage and its 'sweet sounds and harmonies' with the repetitive insistence in line 144 on soli- tude, fear, pain and grief. The passage, like the poem as a whole, works at reassurance through nature, but always there is that same treacher- ous sense of the worryingly disordered state of the world that erupted into 'Lines Written in Early Spring'.

4 Sum up your impressions of the poem as a whole

The full title of the poem is 'Lines written a Few Miles above Tintern Abbey, on Revisiting the Banks of the Wye during a Tour, July 13, 1798', and the opening line dates that first visit as five years earlier in 1793. In 1793, as we have seen, Wordsworth was just back from France in a state of high political and emotional excitement. That mood height- ened his perceptions of the English countryside and gave it a glow that he had warmed himself with for five years. Now he returns to that rec- ollected spot and tries to re-create his experience for Dorothy. Nature with a small *n* is described as a secluded landscape, far from the alien- ating towns, and with a capital *N* as a force underlying the landscape. This force memory and imagination can half-create and then use as a powerful source of pleasure, consolation and moral guidance.

By 1798, Wordsworth needed those things. His confidence in revo- lutionary change in either France or England had ebbed and he had not yet moved on to the orthodox Anglicanism which supplied him with a value system in his later years. He tries to fill the vacuum with nature and Nature: nature's seclusion provides an escape from the world of towns and cities, and Nature can be conjured up to fend off the fear and pain of 'evil tongues' and 'selfish men' (ll. 129–30). In the process of conjuring up that spirit he not only half-creates it but also invests it with religious power, so that the language becomes altogether more solemn and elevated than anywhere else in the *Lyrical Ballads*. The poem itself closes by trying to communicate this way of seeing and believing to Dorothy, who accompanies Wordsworth on his second visit. But the battle to establish this way of seeing sounds across the text. The scatter of exclamations in the closing lines, together with the sense of solitude, fear, grief and pain, subverts his efforts at reassurance, contributing to the poem's status as a tensed, fraught and great Romantic lyric.

Wordsworth wrote most of the poems in *Lyrical Ballads*; of the twenty-three poems in the first, 1798 edition, only four ('The Rime of the Ancient Mariner', 'The Foster-Mother's Tale', 'The Nightingale' and 'The Dungeon') are by Coleridge. What I have aimed to argue is that in his contribution to *Lyrical Ballads* Wordsworth set about mediating the excitement and idealism of the French Revolution into a simple and accessible poetic language. He used that language to celebrate the ordinary pleasures of rural life and rural people, and to some extent to defend that life against the inroads of power in various forms, whether urban, economic, parental or aristocratic. But the battle was being lost, as Wordsworth's letter to Charles James Fox half-acknowledges. So in the collection's concluding poem, 'Tintern Abbey', he sets out to make explicit what has been implicit in many of the ballads: namely, that the imagination and memory, working on selected scenes, can construct out of them a consoling spirit that will at least enable the Wordsworths and others like them to survive as the din and strife of history rolls over them. But we live in history and cannot duck it, and part of the greatness of Wordsworth's poetry is that in the end it faces that fact and the dire tensions it generates.

If you look at any of the poems in *Lyrical Ballads* in the light of these ideas and work on them in the ways I have suggested, you will discover that there is a great deal to say about their concerns, their choice of language, scene and character, and why they are so forceful. At the same time you will start to see why Wordsworth is not just a poet of nature, but, rather, a writer full of complex, anguished thinking about human beings and their lives, both how they are and how they might be. Some of this thinking I have touched on here. It also structures *The Prelude*, the subject of the next chapter.

4

STUDYING WORDSWORTH'S *THE PRELUDE*, BOOKS I AND II

I

THE FIRST, obvious fact about *The Prelude* is that it is a very long narrative poem, whereas so far in this book we have only looked at comparatively short lyrics. This difference in kind means that we shall need to change our method of approach. The tools we have used to analyse a lyric will not work for a narrative poem just because we are dealing with a different kind of work. A sharp knife might be excellent for slicing bread but is not much use when you are trying to dig up the road.

What is a narrative poem? Simply, it is a poem that tells a story. Thus it differs from a lyric, which, as we saw in Chapter 2, usually selects a slight incident or experience and constructs a poem not so much around that incident as around its impact on the poet's thoughts or feelings. Into these two categories, lyric and narrative, you can very broadly subdivide the whole of English poetry.

The Prelude, then, is a narrative poem and the story in it is the story of Wordsworth's early life and its shaping influences. In books I and II, after describing his search for a subject, he moves into an account of his childhood and time at school. The subsequent books continue the story. They tell of his years as a student at Cambridge (books III–VI) and afterwards in London and elsewhere (books VII and VIII). Books IX to XI deal with his residence in France in 1791–2 and his responses to that experience. Those responses, and how he felt his imagination was 'impaired and restored' in the wake of them, are also the subject of the last section of the poem, books XII to XIV. (The book numbers given here correspond to the final, 1850 version of the poem).

So that is the story of *The Prelude.* But the problem is that a narrative poem is never simply reducible to its story. A summary of the plot is sometimes a handy way of tracing the bare bones of a text, but it is no more than that: it does not help us to come to grips with the poet's art. That art starts when the skeleton of the story is fleshed out and brought to life so that it begins to breathe and move in a distinctive way and stops being a mere pile of dry facts. And it is this distinctive life of the text that we are interested in as readers and critics. That truth reminds me of Woody Allen's joke about taking a speed-reading course so that he could get through *War and Peace* in a day. After twenty-four hours his conclusion – 'It's about Russia' – was both correct and useless to the point of absurdity. We could say that, as a narrative poem, *The Prelude* is about Wordsworth's life and we could even go on to list the events he describes, but, without a method that lets us see what is unique and revealing about that story and the poet's construction and reconstruction of it, we should still be left with, at best, an extended version of Woody Allen's banality.

The method that I am going to suggest you use to produce a full analysis is a simplified and very freely adapted version of one first outlined by the French critic Gérard Genette in his book *Narrative Discourse* (Ithaca, NY, 1980). It involves three steps, the first with four subdivisions. That might sound a bit cumbersome, but it is designed to enable you to spot what is important about any of the narrative poems you are likely to meet. In practice you will find that, in a given instance, you will probably draw a blank with one or more of the subdivisions and can focus on the worthwhile material that the others yield. At this stage I shall simply outline the method, and then later in the chapter we shall see what it makes of *The Prelude.*

I Read the poem and try to work out the way the story is patterned

When you read a story that works, whether it is a narrative poem or a novel, it feels 'right' or 'natural' in some mysterious way that you scarcely notice as you are moving through it. One scene appears to lead logically to the next and, as your interest quickens, you seem to be carried along by an inevitable momentum towards the conclusion. That experience is an enjoyable one, and, if all you are looking for is a good read to pass a dull evening, then that is as far as your response will probably go. But, if you want to pass beyond that towards serious literary analysis, you need to think about how the writer organised the text to create that sense of logical inevitability in the reader. There are, broadly, four constituents that can be detected in the organisation of any narrative. They are *order*, *duration*, *frequency* and *point of view*. Let us look at each in turn.

(a)   Order of events

In the real world events occur chronologically and there is nothing we can do about it. What happened at two o'clock on 7 April materialised after what took place at six o'clock on 3 April and incidents in 1964 all came about before 2000. What is almost too trite to notice about life is not, however, true about narrative poetry. There the poet is free to reorganise chronology so that he or she, with the use of flashbacks, jumps, cross-cutting and so on, can present events in a way that is dramatically or ideologically more effective than plodding submission to the iron course of historical sequence. Milton, for example, begins book I of *Paradise Lost* by talking 'Of Mans First Disobedience', but he does not actually get round to describing that disobedience until book IX. The eight intervening books outline what happened before that action, but to focus on the action in the very first line of the poem is to give the following narrative a purpose and a direction that it would otherwise lack. Moments in a text when this sort of reordering of events occurs are moments when most obviously the poet is taking hold of her or his raw material and giving it fresh shape and point. Noticing and analysing those moments will help us to grasp the way the poet is trying to make us view and respond to the story that is being told.

(b)   Duration of events

Again in the real world, events can be timed so as to brook no argument. You can be swept by a mood of poignant delight for a few seconds; the washing-up, especially if you have left it for a bit, can take a solid half hour. But, if you know of a narrative poem that takes a hundred times as many lines to describe the latter experience as the former, I hope you will do the world a favour and burn it before anyone else has to read it. In other words, just as we have seen that poets are not bound by historical sequence, so too they are not bound by historical duration. An incident that was over in a flash can occupy pages and pages in a narrative poem, whereas, equally, intervening years can be passed by in a single line. So, for instance, in Chaucer's *Wife of Bath's Tale* the Wife sets out to tell a story which shows women exercising mastery over men to everyone's advantage, and the narrative is built around that aim. But at one point the knight, the central figure in the story, rapes a maid. The Wife hustles past the crime in a couple of lines. To depict in detail this brute assertion of male dominance would raise issues inconvenient to her tale's moral, so she is quick to pull the reader's attention elsewhere. A trauma that may have changed a woman's whole life flicks past the reader in a second. This sort of manipulation occurs all the time in narrative art as events are stretched or compressed to direct the reader's attention towards what the teller feels is crucial and resonant and elbow it away from the awkward and the irrelevant. If you are alert to that process when you read the narrative, then your understanding of it and its purpose will be immensely enhanced.

(c)   Frequency of events

An old man looking back on fifty years or so of adult life might conclude that in that time there were three or four similar and significant experiences of a special intensity – perhaps of love or of loss, of gain or of insight. He might also care to work out, if he has a calculator handy and has not grown a beard, that he has shaved about 18,250 times. If he then sits down to write an autobiographical narrative poem, I trust, as a potential reader, that he will write a lot about the relatively infrequent loves and losses and very little about the extremely frequent encounters with a razor. To delineate the same event several times, or several similar events, is to signal significance to the reader and as readers we need to respond. So it is that Tennyson's *Idylls of the King*, a series of twelve narrative poems about the adventures of King Arthur and his knights, has duplicated instances of active, malign women, such as Vivien and Guinevere, and duplicated instances of passive, beneficent women, such as Elaine and Enid. Thus a clear and reinforced pattern of values emerges before the reader. Shaving, like the washing-up I mentioned earlier, tends to repeat itself a lot in people's lives but is not normally particularly significant and does not usually feature in a narrative poem. But, when an incident is repeated in a text or where there are a cluster of incidents that obviously belong to the same category, then again we can see the poet's hand at work, foregrounding and highlighting her or his vision of the world. We shall see that vision all the more sharply if we pick up and reflect on those moments of repetition.

(d)   Point of view

One of the first decisions any storyteller has to take concerns the point of view the story will be delivered from. Will it be narrated by one of the participants in the events, and if so which one – a centrally important figure or one of those on the fringes of the action? Or will the narrator be an outsider, an omniscient figure who presides over the whole and can move equally and silently inside and between the minds and hearts of all the actors? The answer to these questions will structure very profoundly what the teller makes of the tale and what he or she elicits from it. There is a particularly good example of what I mean by this in the work of Keats. In his narrative poem *Hyperion*, written in 1818–19, he chooses as his subject the Greek myth of the overthrow of the Titans by a new race of gods. The story is told not by a participant but by an omniscient narrator who effaces himself to describe the reactions of the various defeated Titans. But later in 1819 Keats set about recasting this unfinished poem as *The Fall of Hyperion: A Dream*. In the new work, Keats inserts himself in the text. Writing in the first person, he describes how he falls asleep and sees the Titans' priestess in a dream. It is from her that he learns the fate of the Titans. In the revised poem the Titans' story is made to release quite different meanings, meanings related to the now present Keats and his own processes of discouragement and growth.

What is interesting here is that, by shifting the point of view from third person to first and by putting himself in the poem, Keats makes the same set of events – the fall of the Titans – produce an altered agenda. The later work raises a fresh set of issues because the same catastrophe is being seen from another, more personal vantage point. It is a good illustration of the way that a poet's decision about point of view in a narrative poem will determine the ideas and responses he or she can draw out of the bare facts of the plot. That decision and its implications, therefore, are worth careful attention whenever you are reading a narrative poem.

2   Choose a couple of passages and read them closely to make your impression of the poem more specific

After the first step with its four subdivisions you will begin to have a reasonable impression of the poem, its preoccupations and its direction. This next step will help you bring that impression into finer focus.

Choose a couple of passages that the first step has brought to your attention as possibly significant and pick your way through them to see how,
in more detailed terms, the sensations and reactions that the poem generates in you are provoked. To do this, work particularly with the notion
of choice and combination that we also used when analysing the lyric.
Pause over the actual words the poet deploys to convey the experiences
and look at how those words are combined together to form the text.
Ask yourself how other choices and other combinations might have
made you respond differently and you are half way to defining the
precise effect of the text in front of you. For example, in *The Prelude*
Wordsworth chose to write,

> Bliss was it in that dawn to be alive,
> But to be young was very Heaven!
> (1850 version, XI.108–9)

You could rewrite that as

> Bliss was it in that dawn to be alive,
> But to be young was absolutely ace!

which means more or less the same thing but would provoke a very different response in readers. A poem constructs its readers and their reactions in this fashion with every line. Careful attention to that process in
passages that seem representative will draw you towards a fuller understanding of a given work and its qualities.

3   Sum up your impressions of the poem as a whole

By this stage you will have accumulated quite a lot of material that
touches on various issues. To prevent it looking like a muddled heap
you need, in this final step, to look through it all and give it some concluding shape and point. That will make the entire exercise worthwhile,
because it will leave both you and your reader with a clear sense of your
view of the poem. You do not need to worry if that view contains disparate and even contradictory elements. The Romantic period, as we
saw in the opening chapter, was a disparate and contradictory age, and
texts with the bulk that most narrative poems have will inevitably
encompass some of those blurred tensions. Romantic narrative poetry
speaks to and speaks out of wrenching personal and social discords.

They will prevent you from boiling the poems down to a couple of trite pieties but equally necessitate some attempt at conclusion in order to avoid bewildering, scattered chaos.

II

Before we apply the method to *The Prelude* it will be useful to give the text an anchorage in some sort of context. Briefly, it is a poem about struggles and Wordsworth's attempt to think his way through them to consoling and sustaining sense. These struggles have to be aligned with his changing life if they are to be actively understood.

Wordsworth began *The Prelude* in 1798–9 at Goslar, a small town in Lower Saxony where he spent that winter with his sister Dorothy. Wordsworth never gave the work a proper title. He tended to refer to it as 'the poem to Coleridge', and the name *The Prelude* was chosen by his widow Mary for its first publication in 1850. Her title indicates accurately the poem's status in Wordsworth's own mind: a prelude to what he regarded as his major life's work, a massive three-part philosophical poem on man, nature and society to be called *The Recluse*. Of this only one part (*The Excursion*, 1814) was ever completed, while another fragment (*Home at Grasmere*) was published long after his death.

So *The Prelude* is a prelude to this task, an attempt to examine the resources, capacities and ideas that would equip him to undertake his enormous project. The fact that the project defeated him enables us to see *The Prelude* as in some senses a poem about not being able to write a poem, or rather a poem which shows us that Wordsworth's real interests lay in directions other than the philosophical and social text towards which Coleridge above all urged him. In the cold German winter of 1798–9 he began to write instead 'a Poem on my own earlier life' not just as a prelude to that oppressive task but also as a refuge from it.

In the end *The Prelude* absorbed the best of his creative energies for half a century. *The Recluse* was never finished and instead Wordsworth worked away at the poem on his own earlier life, first expanding it considerably and then again and again revising it, cutting bits, adding bits, altering a word here and a line there. His sense of his own youth and what was important about it changed as he aged and as his values shifted, and the constant rewriting of *The Prelude* is part of the refocusing those changes impelled.

It is important to know from the outset about the revisions to *The Prelude*, although a detailed study of them is best left until later. The most convenient guide to the whole process is the Norton edition of the poem, *William Wordsworth: The Prelude 1799, 1805, 1850*, edited by Jonathan Wordsworth, M.H. Abrams and Stephen Gill (1979). There you will find not only the three main versions of the poem but also a full explanation of their genesis.

Briefly, the first two-part *Prelude*, started in Germany in 1798 and finished in England the following summer, covers more or less the same ground as the first two books of the final version. This 1799 version of the poem was not published until 1974. Wordsworth began working on a second version in 1801. After various changes of plan he finished it in 1805. The original two parts were expanded into thirteen books and took in large, fresh areas of Wordsworth's life – two whole books, for example, on his time in France, and others on his residence at Cambridge and in London, and on his walking tours in the Alps and the Welsh mountains. This text too was not published till our own century, de Selincourt's edition in 1926 being the first. And then there is the final version, usually known as the 1850 *Prelude* because that was when it was published, three months after the poet's death. It was the result of major rewriting in 1816–19, 1832 and again in 1839, which involved, among other things, the splitting of one of the French books into two, so that the 1850 version has fourteen books rather than thirteen. It is important to remember that it is this final 1850 text that is most widely used today and it is likely to be the one you will have to work from if you study the poem. It is therefore the one I use for this chapter.

If we step back and look at the poem Wordsworth left after decades of composition, we can see that it is built around the French Revolution, the formative experience underpinning not just *Lyrical Ballads*, as we noted in the last chapter, but Wordsworth's whole adult life. The point can be proved if you run your eye down the titles of the fourteen books. You will perceive from the titles of the first seven that the first half of the poem moves fairly rapidly through a series of phases in the poet's life: 'Childhood and School-time', 'Residence at Cambridge', 'Summer Vacation', 'Books', 'Cambridge and the Alps', and 'Residence in London'. The eighth book, 'Retrospect', sums up the story so far and prepares us for the core of the text: three books devoted to Wordsworth's period in France in 1791–2 and his view of the French Revolution. The last three books, called 'Imagination and Taste, How Impaired and Restored', 'Imagination and Taste, How Impaired and Restored – Concluded' and 'Conclusion', deal, as their repetitive titles suggest, with Wordsworth's psychological and political devastation in the years after his return from France and how he recovered from that state to his own satisfaction. So it is possible and I think correct to see the whole of *The Prelude* as a build-up to, account of and recovery from the poet's French experience. That is the centre around which the whole work uneasily revolves. Even if you are only studying books I and II, it is necessary to keep that fact at the front of your mind, for reasons that will become clear when we begin to look at those two books more closely.

There is one more useful preliminary concept that an awareness of the whole poem and the process of its making can supply us with before we move on to use the method already outlined as a mode of analysis for books I and II. This concept flows from the famous 'spots of time' passage in book XII of the 1850 version:

> There are in our existence spots of time,
> That with distinct pre-eminence retain
> A renovating virtue, whence, depressed
> By false opinion and contentious thought,
> Or aught of heavier or more deadly weight,
> In trivial occupations, and the round
> Of ordinary intercourse, our minds
> Are nourished and invisibly repaired;
> A virtue, by which pleasure is enhanced,
> That penetrates, enables us to mount,
> When high, more high, and lifts us up when fallen.
>   (XII.208–18)

This is a very complex sentence that demands two or three readings to be properly grasped, but it is worth the effort because in the eyes of many commentators it is the most important passage in *The Prelude*, the one that explains why the work is as it is and not otherwise. Wordsworth argues that there are in our lives moments – 'spots of time' – which possess quite startling power. Memory of them can, to use some of the terms he deploys in this passage, *renovate, nourish, repair, enhance, enable us to mount* and *lift us up*. The reiteration of such terms is evidence of the strength of the signal the poet is trying to transmit.

Now, if we pause for a moment and bend our minds to books I and II, we can suddenly see that they are structured out of a succession of just such 'spots of time'. In book I the spots are bird-snaring and nesting, boat-stealing, skating, fishing, kite-flying and so on. In book II they are experiences such as rowing, riding, flute-music and the setting sun and early-morning walks. They provide the moments, the basic plot if you like, around which the poem is formed.

It is intriguing at this juncture to realise that, in the two-part *Prelude* of 1798–9, the 'spots of time' passage was originally in part I. It is a pity for those who nowadays study only books I and II that Wordsworth moved it, because it provides a key to what can otherwise seem at first glance a string of trivial incidents. The 'spots of time' passage helps us to understand that *The Prelude* is a place where Wordsworth sets about pulling together all those disparate memories of his earlier life from which he has drawn strength in later years in his battles with 'false opinion and contentious thought'. That is why *The Prelude* exists; that is the project that it represents. Wordsworth needed to undertake the project because, as we have already seen, his encounter with revolutionary France fractured his whole process of living and believing, forcing him to rake together and assemble a new set of convictions to put his faith in. *The Prelude* is about that fracturing and reconstructing, an undertaking in which the poet is made to call on all his most potent memories and experiences, his 'spots of time', if he is to avoid disabling depression – what he calls a sense of 'despair' and being 'sick, wearied out with contrarieties' in book XI.

Where have we got to so far in this chapter? Well, we have seen that the writing and rewriting of *The Prelude* absorbs decades of Wordsworth's creative life. The final version moves through his childhood and adolescence towards a full description of his collision with the French Revolution and its splintering impact on his mind and personality. His recovery from that trauma is forged out of the memory of a host of 'spots of time', recollections of incidents in his life from which he derives lasting power and whose description indeed constitutes the bulk of the text. Let us move on to apply the method for reading narrative poetry outlined at the start of this chapter and discover if we can make this brief account a bit more subtle and specific in the case of books I and II.

III

I   Read the poem and try to work out the way the story is patterned

In the last section we looked at the broad arrangement of *The Prelude* as a whole and viewed it as an ascent towards Wordsworth's experience in France, a reconstruction of that French explosion and then a con-cluding account of his recovery. How do the first two books fit into this overall pattern? How do they initiate it? Working with our method enables us to start answering those questions.

(a)   Order of events

The first two books take us from Wordsworth's very earliest memories until the moment when 'my seventeenth year was come' (1850 version, II.386), but there are two significant deviations from that progression. First, there is the long section at the beginning of the poem which is situated in the present rather than the past and which means that the ostensible subject of book I, namely 'Childhood and School-time', is not really engaged with until more than two-fifths of the way through the book. And, secondly, there are the frequent subsequent occasions when the poet suspends the story of his childhood and its events in order to ponder and explain to the reader the importance that those incidents hold for him now as he writes and remembers.

What these breaks in chronological order mean is that the poem opens not with some dim, infant recollection but with a compelling burst of joy expressing the poet's present happiness, as in the exclama-tion in the very first line: 'O there is a blessing in this gentle breeze'. The reader is thus led into the poem breathing an atmosphere of happy release as the poet returns to 'green fields' (I.4) and escapes from an unnamed, imprisoning 'vast city' (I.7). It is through this entrance that we approach Wordsworth's following recital of his childhood experi-ences, and so are made to read them as part of the same process of self-restoration. This idea is strengthened towards the end of book II, when again strict chronology is breached and the poet jumps forward from his seventeenth year to the present, to this 'melancholy waste of hopes o'erthrown' (II.433), a period of 'dereliction and dismay' (II.441). The reference here is to the collapse of those inchoate expectations that the French Revolution had at first inspired in Wordsworth and many others. But this forlorn and desperate mood is made bearable by Nature, which has proved to be a 'never-failing principle of joy' (II.450) amidst the sneers, the apathy and the selfishness of those times.

So at once we can perceive the ordering principle that underlies *The Prelude*. Cutting through the narrative of Wordsworth's life and pro-viding a justification for it is a celebration of the nourishment he has derived from his contacts with nature and his memories of such con-tacts right from infancy. This nourishment can take the simple form of a feeling of renewal after quitting the constrictions of the city, but also the more profound form of a source of sustaining consolation in the face of such things as political despair, personal depression and social alienation. The elaboration of this 'never-failing principle of joy' into a fundamental philosophy of life is the project of *The Prelude*.

(b)   Duration of events

There is one passage in these first two books where it seems to me that Wordsworth very evidently stops the story and spends a significantly extended time pausing over one point. It is the long section in book I, running for over a hundred lines (ll. 146–269), where he reviews possible subjects for a major poem and his inhibiting difficulties with all of them. It is, if you think about it, an odd thing to do, to spend a considerable time writing about matters you are not going to be writing about. You might expect a list of rejected alternatives to survive as far as the first draft but probably no further, and yet here they are filling nearly a fifth of the first book even after the lifetime of revision that went into the making of *The Prelude*. Why?

A clue emerges if we run through the list. Again and again the topics that beckon the poet are stories of fights against oppression. These can be 'dire enchantments faced and overcome' (I.175), fables of 'wrongs to redress' (I.182) or even the overthrow of the Roman Empire (I.190). They are legends of the survival of liberty in 'tyrannic times' (I.203), tales of how Dominique de Gourges in Florida or Gustavus in Sweden or Wallace in Scotland roamed about 'withering the Oppressor' (I.212). But, whenever he tried to work any of these subjects up into a poem, 'I recoil and droop' (I.265), and in that mood of failure he succumbs to other temptations:

> Ah! better far than this, to stray about
> Voluptuously through fields and rural walks,
> And ask no record of the hours, resigned
> To vacant musing. . . .
>
>   (I.250–3)

It is clear here that what Wordsworth's creative capacities slide away from are accounts of the same sort of massive social and political struggles that he had witnessed in France. Instead, what both he and his imagination are drawn towards is something more solitary and private: it is nature-centred ('fields and rural walks') and works with the random

thoughts, the 'vacant musing', that straying through such scenes pro-
vokes. And it is there that the 'philosophic song/Of Truth that cherishes
our daily life' (I.299–30) that he yearns to write will at last be found.
Such truth, he comes to believe, lies not in the great themes of nationalist battles for independence or the popular rising against a tyrant but
in private experience, especially contact with the natural world, and an
unforced attempt to ponder on and draw strength from that experience.

Thus it is that, working his way through his own false starts,
Wordsworth arrives at the idea that explodes into his fourteen-book
autobiography. The false starts remain there in this final version of *The
Prelude* not as strangely surviving relics of the poem's genesis but rather
as a central pillar of its ultimate meaning. Together with the three later
books on France they consitute Wordsworth's deliberate marking out
of the space where, in his increasingly conservative view, truth and personal fulfilment are *not* to be found. His imagination recoils from the
exploits of, say, Gustavus in the same way as his whole personality col-
lapses after the turmoil of France. The path is opened for a poem that
hunts for sources of strength in other, more secluded places.

(c)   Frequency of events

We can track down those sources most easily if we look at the kind of
material Wordsworth fills his text with in the absence of Gustavus and
the rest. The poet himself describes the nature of that material plainly
enough at the beginning of book II:

> Thus far, O Friend! have we, though leaving much
> Unvisited, endeavoured to retrace
> The simple ways in which my childhood walked;
> Those chiefly that first led me to the love
> Of rivers, woods, and fields.
>
> (II.1–5)

Reflection on this extract prompts two comments. First, we are
reminded of the enormous proportion of a text that Wordsworth
was still tinkering with in his seventies that is given over to childhood
memories. And, second, it is striking that they are childhood memories
of a very particular sort, centred on 'rivers, woods, and fields'. After
all, another and perhaps more common form of boyhood recollection
would be dominated by other people: by the massive presence of
parents, for example, and other looming adults, or perhaps by other

children and all the terrors and raptures that can stem from brothers and sisters.

To turn to our infancy is of course to turn to a formative part of our lives. But it is a part that in many cases, as in Wordsworth's, is blocked off from the even more formative experiences of the adult, from the glum problems of day-to-day economic survival to the ecstatic shambles of sexuality. Wordsworth did indeed include a coded rendering of his love affair with Annette Vallon in the story of Vaudracour and Julia in book IX, but he cut it from the final version of the poem.

So what we are left with, especially in books I and II, is a very singular account of childhood. Other children and adults are certainly there, but faded to a point where none of them is ever personalised to the extent of being named. And if you examine the events that go to make up the two books, then again and again you will see that the reader's attention is directed to moments when Wordsworth is alone. Not all the experiences in these first two books are lonely ones: he walks and rides and plays cards with his companions, but always the instant of highlighted significance is solitary. When he snares the birds 'I was alone' (I.315) and when he climbs to their nests 'I hung alone' (I.336). There is 'solitude' (I.394) during and after his theft of the boat, and more 'solitude' (I.422) in the course of his November ramblings through a 'lonely scene' (I.418). Even when part of a group his inclination is to withdraw, leaving the 'tumultuous throng' of skaters (I.449) and learning even while rowing with his fellows the 'self-sufficing power of Solitude' (II.77). 'Solitude' he finds 'more active even than "best society"' (II.294–5), so that he is happy to 'walk alone, / Under the quiet stars' (II.302–3) or sit 'Alone upon some jutting eminence' (II.343). Unsurprisingly, then, it is a tribute to Coleridge's search for 'truth in solitude' (II.461) that brings book II to a conclusion.

These and other similar references are too frequent to be coincidental. True, the same plain rural pleasures that we saw being celebrated in *Lyrical Ballads* are being gathered together here. Intense and lasting delight comes from simple incidents on a walk or a ride, climbing a hill or rowing a boat, not from the sophisticated pastimes of the city the poet has abandoned or the 'smart Assembly-room' with its screaming fiddles that he shudders away from at the start of book II. But the striking new element is the insistence on the loneliness of these renovating moments, the need to pursue them away from 'the haunts of men' (II.468) and to search for peace and truth in solitude.

Such movements of shy retreat or hurt withdrawal are common enough in our own day, especially for those whose economic means or social position gives them the necessary space for such a manoeuvre. What is enormously significant is to see Wordsworth tracing out that movement in the very generation when, as we noted in the opening chapter, the world's first predominantly urban and industrial society was beginning to be drilled and fastened into place. The wounded spirit flees from the city at the outset of the poem, and at the core of the poem the mature adult writes off his engagement with sexuality and with revolutionary politics in France as post-adolescent folly. And so the way is clear for an attempt to piece together a survival strategy from the shreds and fragments of solitary experience, treated as sacred because they are held to proceed from unspoilt nature and are consumed privately without the tainting contact of other people. What is mapped out in *The Prelude* is thus a conservative route towards personal fulfilment in an alien and alienating society.

(d)   Point of view

If what I have said is true, then Wordsworth's choice of a point of view in *The Prelude* becomes unavoidable. A first-person narrative centres the text unambiguously where its prime interest is to be found; namely, to quote its sub-title, in 'The Growth of a Poet's Mind: An Autobiographical Poem'. To some extent, of course, a first-person narrative is the obvious way to write an autobiography, although it is not inevitable. Thomas Hardy, for example, also wrote the story of his own life in two books called *The Early Life of Thomas Hardy* and *The Later Years of Thomas Hardy* but cast them in the third person, as though the events were being observed and described by someone else.

But for Wordsworth the choice of the first person as his narrative mode fits perfectly with what we have begun to see as the main project of *The Prelude*. Look at the moment in book I when he finally sets aside his failures to make a poem out of history and legend and turns to face his own life:

> Was it for this
> That one, the fairest of all rivers, loved
> To blend his murmurs with my nurse's song,
> And, from his alder shades and rocky falls,
> And from his fords and shallows, sent a voice
> That flowed along my dreams?
>
> (I.269–74)

We can watch the poet doing two things at once here. First, and simply, he is recounting his earliest infant memories of the 1770s by the River Derwent. But at the same time the narrator is taking hold of those memories and pondering their significance ('Was it for this . . .?') for him now as he writes half a lifetime later. So the poem becomes not just a straightforward account of past experiences but rather a sifting of those experiences in the present, scrutinising them for their worth and connotations. For that sort of project clearly the uniquely privileged access which a first-person narrator has both to the facts of the subject's past and to the beliefs of his present is an essential part of the structuring of the text.

2   Choose a couple of passages and read them closely to make your impression of the poem more specific

We have arrived, then, at the point where we can see *The Prelude* doing two principal things: first, re-creating past experiences or 'spots of time' as Wordsworth calls them; and, secondly, drawing back and teasing out the subsequent meaning and value of those moments. I have chosen for closer inspection a couple of passages which embody those two characteristic elements in the poem.

First, the spot of time:

And in the frosty season, when the sun
Was set, and visible for many a mile
The cottage windows blazed through twilight gloom,
I heeded not their summons: happy time
It was indeed for all of us – for me
It was a time of rapture! Clear and loud
The village clock tolled six, – I wheeled about,
Proud and exulting like an untired horse
That cares not for his home. All shod with steel,
We hissed along the polished ice in games
Confederate, imitative of the chase
And woodland pleasures, – the resounding horn,
The pack loud chiming, and the hunted hare.
So through the darkness and the cold we flew,
And not a voice was idle; with the din
Smitten, the precipices rang aloud;

The leafless trees and every icy crag
Tinkled like iron; while far distant hills
Into the tumult sent an alien sound
Of melancholy not unnoticed, while the stars
Eastward were sparkling clear, and in the west
The orange sky of evening died away.
Not seldom from the uproar I retired
Into a silent bay, or sportively
Glanced sideway, leaving the tumultuous throng,
To cut across the reflex of a star
That fled, and, flying still before me, gleamed
Upon the glassy plain; and oftentimes,
When we had given our bodies to the wind,
And all the shadowy banks on either side
Came sweeping through the darkness, spinning still
The rapid line of motion, then at once
Have I, reclining back upon my heels,
Stopped short; yet still the solitary cliffs
Wheeled by me – even as if the earth had rolled
With visible motion her diurnal round!
Behind me did they stretch in solemn train,
Feebler and feebler, and I stood and watched
Till all was tranquil as a dreamless sleep.

                                        (I.425–63)

Wordsworth typically begins this re-creation of the experience of skating as a child with a description of the natural context: the frosty season, the setting sun and the twilight gloom. That context keeps on reasserting itself through the subsequent lines so that it is never simply a vague background but becomes part of the experience itself, with the 'leafless trees', the 'orange sky' and the 'shadowy banks' as central to the memory as the physical exhilaration of skating.

In this context

                              happy time
It was indeed for all of us – for me
It was a time of rapture!

In a familiar move Wordsworth here both locates himself as part of the group – 'us' – and then distinguishes his reaction from that of the others. This pattern repeats itself throughout the extract, so that 'we' are 'confederate' and like a 'pack', making a communal 'din' and 'tumult' between lines 433 and 446. But then in line 447 'I retired' into a moment of private silence. Or again, when 'we had given our bodies to the wind' (l. 453), then 'I . . . Stopped short' by the 'solitary cliffs'. These withdrawals into self prepare for the dizzy illusion that the paragraph works towards as its conclusion: the very earth itself appears to revolve around the stopped, silent 'I'.

This is a well-known passage in *The Prelude* and you have perhaps come across tributes to its technical skill – the way, for example, that Wordsworth builds up the momentum of the speeding pack in a dozen or more lines, most of them run-on, and then the lines, like the skater himself, are stopped short with the heavy caesuras of lines 458 and 459 and the exclamation mark in line 460. But what is worth noting as much as the technical deftness of the piece is its emphasis on material objects. Wordsworth is not betrayed into facile poeticisms in his attempt to convey a moment of high exaltation. Instead, the words remain in close touch with the concrete substantialities of the context, right from the initial precision of the village clock and its six tolls. Then it is all ice and steel and iron, hills and stars, banks and cliffs, trees and crags, as the solid facts of the place are stamped into our minds, largely without the dilution of falsely prettifying adjectives. Only at the spinning conclusion does all that hard materiality begin to dissolve and become 'Feebler and feebler' as the poet whirls into a state of abstraction, 'tranquil as a dreamless sleep'. The strength of this passage, and of all the finest 'spots of time', is the way Wordsworth uses 'the real language of men' that he had championed in the *Lyrical Ballads* Preface to elicit from the solid actualities of everyday life and experience their latent, vivid power.

The second passage I have chosen for closer inspection is one in which Wordsworth steps back from the spots of time to ponder their meaning and value:

> 'Twere long to tell
> What spring and autumn, what the winter snows,
> And what the summer shade, what day and night,
> Evening and morning, sleep and waking thought,
> From sources inexhaustible, poured forth
> To feed the spirit of religious love
> In which I walked with Nature. But let this
> Be not forgotten, that I still retained
> My first creative sensibility;

That by the regular action of the world
My soul was unsubdued. A plastic power
Abode with me; a forming hand, at times
Rebellious, acting in a devious mood;
A local spirit of his own, at war
With general tendency, but, for the most,
Subservient strictly to external things
With which it communed. An auxiliar light
Came from my mind, which on the setting sun
Bestowed new splendour; the melodious birds,
The fluttering breezes, fountains that ran on
Murmuring so sweetly in themselves, obeyed
A like dominion, and the midnight storm
Grew darker in the presence of my eye:
Hence my obeisance, my devotion hence,
And hence my transport.

                                         (II.352–76)

This extract begins by alluding to a mass of potential spots of time amid
'the winter snows' and 'the summer shade', and it touches on others at
the end: 'the setting sun' and 'the midnight storm', for example. But
in the main the passage is not concerned to describe those incidents but
is concerned rather to analyse the nature of their impact on the poet.
At this point Wordsworth uses again the idea we noticed in 'Tintern
Abbey' in the last chapter, the idea that we do not passively reflect the
world in our minds but 'half-create' what we see. This ability is vari-
ously described here as 'My first creative sensibility', 'My soul,' 'A plastic
power', 'a forming hand', 'A local spirit', 'An auxiliar light' and 'my
eye'. The pile of synonyms marks Wordsworth's anxiety to get the
concept across to the reader. It is this power and sensibility, this imagination, to add another synonym, that really constitutes experience, that
takes hold of the myriad objects which cluster in the spots of time and
arranges them in patterns of consoling significance. And it is this insistence on, and exercise of, humanity's creative capacities that can make
the reading of the finest parts of *The Prelude* an intoxicating and wholly
liberating encounter.

     The next point that strikes me about this passage, especially by con-
trast with the first one we looked at, is the realisation that hard materiality has given way to a drift of soft abstract nouns: *thought, sources,
love, Nature, sensibility, action, power, mood, tendency, splendour, dominion,
presence, obeisance, devotion, transport.* How we fill and define and under-

stand those terms is problematic for a reader in a way that, for example, ice and steel and crags were not in the previous passage. The 'real language of men' has plainly been laid aside for an altogether different and more difficult discourse.

Perhaps the key phrase in the passage concerns the poet's sense of the 'spirit of religious love / In which I walked with Nature', a phrase that survives unchanged in the 1850 version from the first 1798–9 draft. The Wordsworth of that winter was a man in retreat from radical politics and a man distanced from orthodox Christianity. What we can see him doing is working to create a belief system of his own, apart from the actualities of politics or the consolations of the Church. And so his own sensibility, power, soul, light, spirit – the repetition underlines the intensity of the strain – is being forced with unremitting application to make out of his experiences with nature a sustaining 'spirit of religious love'. The clouds of abstractions that effort blows up are further evidence of the intensity of that effort, even if they end by obscuring the solution. The frequency with which Wordsworth went back to *The Prelude* and reworked and rewrote it is perhaps a sign of his own acknowledgement of that fact. The deep, continuing struggle breaks through in the very terms he chooses to describe the process: *unsubdued, rebellious, devious, at war with general tendency.*

3 Sum up your impressions of the poem as a whole

Looking back across the ideas we have gathered together in this chapter we can offer one or two conclusions about *The Prelude* and the kind of project that it represents. We have seen Wordsworth at the start of book I turning to nature with a small *n* in a mood of delighted relief after the constrictions of the city, and then, in a sharply ideological move, turning at the end of book II to Nature with a capital *N* as a quasi-religious source of consolation in depressing times. He arrives at this autobiographical subject matter after failing to find inspiration in myth and history, the traditional sources for long narrative poems. From that failure he slides by implicit deduction to the conviction that a sustaining philosophy can be derived, not from the usual grand themes, but rather from our own remembered experiences, those normally solitary 'spots of time' whose profound truth will be revealed by the careful re-creating and meditating that fills much of the poem. In this sense we can read *The Prelude* as Wordsworth's attempt to solve the contradictions we noted him confronting with anguish in *Lyrical Ballads* – his pleasure in nature against his grief at 'What man has made of man' in 'Lines Written in Early Spring', or his veneration of Nature intercut with his shrinking in the face of the 'dreary intercourse of daily life' in 'Tintern Abbey'.

It is for this reason that the memories assembled in *The Prelude* are not just the rambling reminiscences of an old man, of interest only to himself. Rather, as revealed by the two passages we have looked at, moments such as skating one distant winter evening are reconstructed by Wordsworth in graphic and concrete detail because those moments are deployed in the poem as the foundations of a proffered philosophy of life. They are moments when in some half-conscious way he feels he has been touched by the consoling and invigorating power of Nature. So the purpose of the poem is both to conjure up those moments and to think through to their significance, thus generating what he calls near the end of book II 'a faith / That fails not' (ll. 443–4) both for himself and his readers.

If you stop and consider it, it is a huge and creditable undertaking to try to forge out of the incidental bits and pieces of your own life a set of beliefs that will fulfil the same sort of function as traditional religion and that will sustain not just yourself but later generations facing a 'melancholy waste of hopes o'erthrown' (II.433), the collapse of political dreams and social ideas. The size and the strain of the task and the contradictions within it are what eventually stall it. In *The Prelude* Wordsworth's characteristic movement is towards the lonely and the solitary. His instinct is to be a recluse; and yet in the end *The Recluse* defeated him and was never written, as we saw earlier.

The alternative to that seclusion is the working and loving and struggling with other men and women to build a better world together that exhilarated Wordsworth in France, that is stunningly caught in the central section of *The Prelude*, but that he lost touch with after his return to England. Instead, language and imagination are pressed to their very limits in a search for what 'Tintern Abbey' calls with desperate vagueness a 'something far more deeply interfused', a something that Wordsworth vainly hunts for in *The Prelude* through all those frustratingly imprecise abstractions. The greatness of *The Prelude* perhaps lies in that very failure, in the way that it enables us both to watch the construction of a still commonly available mode of thinking and believing and to glimpse its limitations and defeats, its negations and its gaps. Indeed, the very length of the poem, with its repeated circling around similar incidents, and the fact that so many of these incidents seem problematic rather than simply uplifting, indicates the extent to which

Wordsworth himself was aware of the strains and breaks inherent in his enterprise. He had too much integrity and intelligence not to know that the philosophy of retreat and communion with nature that he was striving to develop was wide open to doubts and questions. Meanwhile the 'hunger-bitten girl', whom we saw Wordsworth with awkward honesty including in book IX, still waits with a silent rebuke that calls clamorously for action.

5

TACKLING A
COLERIDGE POEM

I

WORDSWORTH and Coleridge tend to go together and there are good reasons for this pairing apart from the obvious one of their joint production of *Lyrical Ballads*. Like Wordsworth, Coleridge was born into relative middle-class comfort, the youngest son of John Coleridge, Vicar of Ottery St Mary in Devon, and his wife Anne, née Bowden. Like Wordsworth he went to Cambridge, and like Wordsworth and indeed most young people of the time with a grain of idealism he was stirred by the revolutionary enthusiasms of the early 1790s.

Whilst at Cambridge, Coleridge devoured the work of radical thinkers such as Voltaire, Paine, Godwin and Wollstonecraft and won a medal for a poem against the slave trade. He moved away from establishment Anglicanism and was nearly thrown out of the university for his support of William Frend, a Jesus College Fellow banished from Cambridge for writing a Unitarian pamphlet that the Vice-Chancellor regarded as seditious. In 1794 Coleridge met Robert Southey, an Oxford student expelled from his public school for writing an article against corporal punishment, and together they dreamed of 'pantisocracy'. The word was coined by Coleridge to describe a utopian community in which power and produce would be shared equally amongst all its members. They planned to establish this community in the eastern United States on the banks of the Susquehanna with a dozen or so like-minded couples. To this end Southey was engaged to a Bristol woman, Edith Fricker, and persuaded Coleridge to get engaged to her sister Sara.

And so we could go on, constructing for Coleridge the same sort of biography of a young man in revolt that we made for Wordsworth. Amongst his earliest published poems were twelve 'Sonnets on Eminent Characters' contributed to the oppositional *Morning Chronicle* in December 1794 and January 1795. These included an exclamatory attack on the Prime Minister, Pitt, as well as warm praise for such radical heroes as Godwin and Southey. In Bristol in 1795 we find him upsetting local Tories with a fiery series of lectures which he promptly published. These aimed to raise money to finance pantisocracy, and their various targets included the Government, the slave trade, the war against France and the amassing of private fortunes.

All of this work took energy, courage and commitment that we need to insist on in the face of subsequent critics, the older Coleridge sadly among them, who prefer to sidle past it either with embarrassed silence or a condescending scoff. True, there are immature elements of playing at revolution in it all, as fatuous talk of seeking a 'cottag'd dell' to dance a 'moonlight roundelay' in Coleridge's 1794 poem 'Pantisocracy' suggests. And there is too the odd business of his drunken decision in 1793 to enlist in the 15th Light Dragoons under the name of Silas Tomkyn Comberbache. After a couple of months he was tracked down and bought out by his brother George; but, as more than one commentator has noted, it was a strange place for an opponent of the war against France to go to hide from his debts. What in fact emerges, as it emerged in Wordsworth's case, is a sense of a young man torn between, on the one hand, the conditioning of his class and education, which directed him towards defensive, complacent privilege, and, on the other, the exhilarating pull of revolutionary ideals which challenged that conditioning and offered braver, wider possibilities. It was just such a young man, still only twenty-two, who married Sara Fricker in 1795 and who around the same time wrote 'The Eolian Harp'.

II

I have chosen to start with 'The Eolian Harp' because it is the first of what have become known as Coleridge's 'conversation poems'. These poems, which include 'Reflections on Having Left a Place of Retirement', 'This Lime-tree Bower my Prison', 'Frost at Midnight', 'Fears in Solitude' and 'The Nightingale', as well as 'The Eolian Harp', form a distinctively Coleridgean achievement, a group of discursive lyrics in which the poet both observes and meditates out loud as he addresses a

silent listener. Working with the sense of the young Coleridge that we
have just established and the method for analysing a lyric described in
Chapter 2, let us see what we can make of 'The Eolian Harp'.

My pensive Sara! thy soft cheek reclined
Thus on mine arm, most soothing sweet it is
To sit beside our Cot, our Cot o'ergrown
With white-flower'd Jasmin, and the broad-leav'd Myrtle,
(Meet emblems they of Innocence and Love!)   5
And watch the clouds, that late were rich with light,
Slow saddening round, and mark the star of eve
Serenely brilliant (such should Wisdom be)
Shine opposite! How exquisite the scents
Snatch'd from yon bean-field! and the world *so* hush'd!   10
The stilly murmur of the distant Sea
Tells us of silence.

                    And that simplest Lute,
Placed length-ways in the clasping casement, hark!
How by the desultory breeze caress'd,   15
Like some coy maid half yielding to her lover,
It pours such sweet upbraiding, as must needs
Tempt to repeat the wrong! And now, its strings
Boldlier swept, the long sequacious notes
Over delicious surges sink and rise,   20
Such a soft floating witchery of sound
As twilight Elfins make, when they at eve
Voyage on gentle gales from Fairy-Land,
Where Melodies round honey-dropping flowers,
Footless and wild, like birds of Paradise;   25
Nor pause, nor perch, hovering on untam'd wing!
O! the one Life within us and abroad,
Which meets all motion and becomes its soul,
A light in sound, a sound-like power in light,
Rhythm in all thought, and joyance every where –   30
Methinks, it should have been impossible
Not to love all things in a world so fill'd;
Where the breeze warbles, and the mute still air
Is Music slumbering on her instrument.
    And thus, my Love! as on the midway slope   35
Of yonder hill I stretch my limbs at noon,
Whilst through my half-clos'd eye-lids I behold

The sunbeams dance, like diamonds, on the main,
And tranquil muse upon tranquillity;
Full many a thought uncall'd and undetain'd,   40
And many idle flitting phantasies,
Traverse my indolent and passive brain,
As wild and various as the random gales
That swell and flutter on this subject Lute!
  And what if all of animated nature   45
Be but organic Harps diversely fram'd,
That tremble into thought, as o'er them sweeps
Plastic and vast, one intellectual breeze,
At once the Soul of each, and God of all?
  But thy more serious eye a mild reproof   50
Darts, O beloved Woman! nor such thoughts
Dim and unhallow'd dost thou not reject,
And biddest me walk humbly with my God.
Meek Daughter in the family of Christ!
Well hast thou said and holily disprais'd   55
These shapings of the unregenerate mind;
Bubbles that glitter as they rise and break
On vain Philosophy's aye-babbling spring.
For never guiltless may I speak of him,
The Incomprehensible! save when with awe   60
I praise him, and with Faith that inly *feels*;
Who with his saving mercies healéd me,
A sinful and most miserable man,
Wilder'd and dark, and gave me to possess
Peace, and this Cot, and thee, heart-honour'd Maid!   65

I Look for the main idea or feeling

If we begin by remembering the notion of tensions, hopes and fears that
we used earlier in the book, we can I think see how this poem builds
its tensions clearly into its very structure. The poem is divided into five
verse paragraphs and opens by addressing the poet's wife: 'My pensive
Sara!' Coleridge's line of thought is then developed through the next
three paragraphs. All of them open with a simple co-ordinating conjunction – 'And that simplest Lute', 'And thus, my Love!', 'And what
if' – as the poet's mind wanders and he conceptualises freely. But then
the flow is checked, 'And' gives way to a contradictory 'But', and in the
last paragraph Sara appears to halt the speculation:

But thy more serious eye a mild reproof
Darts, O beloved Woman!

That 'But' becomes the point of reversal in the poem. Before it, the
poet in the first paragraph observes the natural beauty of a Somerset
evening; in the second he listens and imaginatively reacts to the sounds
made by the breeze on a wind harp hanging in the window; by the third
and fourth paragraph he is moved to wonder if his 'indolent and passive
brain' is not like the harp, solicited into beautiful response by a mysterious force which is 'At once the Soul of each, and God of all?' But
then all of this free-thinking is swept aside by an admonitory final
paragraph which insists on an orthodox notion of God as 'The Incomprehensible', not to be reached by the vain philosophising proceeding
from the 'unregenerate mind' of a 'sinful and most miserable man'.
Plainly a central tension in the lyric is between a mind prone to
theorise boldly about the profoundest truths and one that starts like a
guilty thing at such a prospect and withdraws into a humble and self-
denigrating faith.

2   Look at the choices and combinations of words that express the main idea or feeling

If we move closer to the terms Coleridge uses to convey the tension in
the text, what strikes me at once is the sensuous extravagance of the
first four paragraphs when compared with the constrained severity of
the last sixteen lines. Indeed, the opening lines are filled with a series
of calculated appeals to the five senses which might remind us of Keats's
odes, So, in addition to the murmur of the sea in the first paragraph,
there is the sustained attempt in the second to imitate the sound of the
lute, which comes through particularly in that repeated alliterative 's'
in lines 16–20 as the wind hisses across the strings. Taste is primed by
the 'honey-dropping flowers' in line 24, and there is the flickering touch
of the 'soft cheek . . . on mine arm' at the start as well as the caresses
of the breeze in line 15. Our sense of smell is stimulated by the 'exquisite . . . scents' in line 9, while the whole of the first paragraph works on
our sense of sight, as we sit with Coleridge and Sara and 'watch the
clouds' of the evening thickening round their cottage garden. And at
the same time, throughout the first forty-eight lines, the poet keeps
slipping from these sensuous experiences into a chain of 'flitting phantasies' – from the 'coy maid' and the 'birds of Paradise' in the second

paragraph, for example, to musing about the nature of the universe and the deity in the fourth.

But after the 'reproof' in line 50 this process halts. The union of sensuous response and brave free-thinking of the first four paragraphs is dismissed in a belittling phrase ('vain Philosophy's aye-babbling spring') and the language of traditional Christian piety dominates: *unhallow'd, humbly, Meek, Christ, holily, unregenerate, never guiltless, The Incomprehensible, awe, praise, Faith, saving mercies, sinful, Peace*. A restrained, orthodox discourse is put in place as an explicit reprimand to the substance of the first three-quarters of the lyric, where immediate feeling was used as a spontaneous way into imagining and elaborating a system of personal belief. Sara may direct us at the end towards meek faith, but the poet himself sings more eagerly of the world and its sharp materiality.

3   Focus on the lines which clinch your sense of the poem's main idea or feeling

We have already seen that the poem turns on the opening of the final paragraph, so it is worth looking closely at the way Coleridge negotiates that transition:

> But thy more serious eye a mild reproof
> Darts, O beloved Woman! nor such thoughts
> Dim and unhallow'd dost thou not reject,
> And biddest me walk humbly with my God.

These lines are a tangle. We have to pause and translate the double negative ('nor such thoughts . . . dost thou not reject') into a positive statement, a move not helped by the fact that there is a third negative ('unhallow'd') in between the first two. It is a backwards sort of tactic to introduce what is supposed to be a positive conclusion to the lyric. And then there is the fact that Sara, the 'beloved Woman', is used to deliver the rebuke. It is fruitless to speculate whether Sara did actually reprove Coleridge at this point or whether this is just a fictional device. But what is certainly significant for readers of the text is that the shift is as it were externalised: it is not part of the poet's own instinctive mental development which we have followed, but is instead presented as a check to that development originating outside the poet and his consciousness. With a single directive phrase – 'And biddest me walk humbly with my God' – it draws him back to the same childlike expression of Christian dogma that we shall find at the end of 'The Rime of the Ancient Mariner'. In short, the terms Coleridge uses to establish this moment of transition tend in an odd but revealing way to undermine its credibility.

4   Sum up your impressions of the poem as a whole

Coleridge's first conversation poem seems to revolve around a sharp tension between two kinds of belief. The first set of beliefs is described as arising from the poet's personal, sensuous responses, which the text details and which flow naturally into free speculation about subjects as diverse as mythical birds and notions of God. Then, having spent three-quarters of the poem indulging this process, the lyric goes awkwardly into reverse, condemns these 'vain babblings' and accepts Sara's insistence on a different belief system, one based not on thought but on 'Faith that inly *feels*'. As a further complication, it is worth noting that at this point Coleridge originally added a footnote in French, a quotation from 'Citoyenne Roland' outlining her sympathetic if critical view of atheism. Madame Roland was a leading figure in the French Revolution. Her husband was a member of the Government after the overthrow of King Louis XVI, and she was guillotined less than two years before the poem was written, when the party she and her husband supported, the Girondins, were ousted from power.

What I think we have in 'The Eolian Harp' is a document full of the tensions and the contradictions of the early 1790s. There is the daring and uninhibited speculation of the first forty-eight lines. That is cut across by a voice, not Coleridge's but ascribed to Sara, that reasserts traditional faith. But that too is deflected by another voice, again not Coleridge's but Madame Roland's, buried in a footnote later suppressed, that breathes the heady air of revolutionary France. The whole is orchestrated by Coleridge, the Anglican vicar's son who became a radical Unitarian, the passionate lecturer against the French war who briefly joined the British army, the dreamer of pantisocratic dreams who survives in our own day as one of the forerunners of conservative philosophy. While he lived and wrote out of those contradictions he was a major poet; when he later lost touch with them the poet in him dried up.

III

In the autumn of 1797, two years after completing 'The Eolian Harp', Coleridge began to write 'The Rime of the Ancient Mariner'. In some ways little had changed in those two years. He was still living in the same district, though he had moved a few miles west to Nether Stowey. His marriage to Sara was still relatively happy and not shaken by the storms that were to make it impossible for them both in later years. He remained in contact with radical politics, being visited at Nether Stowey by, for example, the revolutionary John Thelwall and hence being reported on by a Government spy. Yet at the same time he continued to edge his way back towards a prudent conservatism, as the last lines of his 1796 'Ode to the Departing Year' suggest.

But there was one crucial change in Coleridge's life in those two years: his regular contact with Wordsworth, who moved into Alfoxden, only four miles from Nether Stowey, in July 1797. The kind of political stimulation that we have seen Coleridge receiving earlier in the decade from Southey he now found as a poet from Wordsworth, and they at once began to plan their joint venture *Lyrical Ballads*. The longest and the first work in that volume was Coleridge's narrative poem 'The Rime of the Ancient Mariner'. Let us see how far the method for reading narrative poetry outlined in the last chapter can take us in understanding this ballad (unfortunately too long to print here, but available in most anthologies of English poetry).

I Read the poem and try to work out the way the story is patterned

(a) Order of events

The main thing to notice about the order of events in the poem is the odd fact that the story starts after it has finished. In other words, we do not begin at the chronologically earliest point, with the Mariner setting out on his voyage, but rather we open with twenty lines which describe a scene long after the end of the journey when the Mariner seizes hold of the Wedding-Guest and prepares to tell him his tale. We are reminded of this reluctant listener at several points in the ballad. He interrupts, for example, at the end of part I and at the beginning of part IV, and the poem concludes with eight stanzas that take us back again to the wedding. The obvious question is, why does Coleridge choose to do this? Why does he frame his fantastic narrative with the wedding of an unnamed couple who having nothing at all to do with the story? Why a man on the way into a feast as the recipient of the account rather than, say, a child on the way to school or a woman on the way to a pub?

What I think this particular frame does for readers of the poem is to dramatise the Mariner's separation from normal, convivial humanity. The first two stanzas tell us that the guest is one of a group of three, next of kin to the groom, who has thrown open his door to welcome the trio to the feast with its 'merry din'. The ancient, skinny Mariner, the grey-beard loon with the glittering eye, is a creature set apart from all that communal jollity. He pulls the Wedding-Guest and by implication us, his readers, aside from the cheerful mainstream to voyage in perilous waters. By the time we rejoin that mainstream at the end with its 'loud uproar' (l. 591) we are perhaps ready like the Guest to turn away sadder and wiser. We are no longer drawn by the fatuous merriment but have learned to see the world for a while through the eyes of the excluded and the persecuted, the lonely and the spurned. In that sense the wedding-feast framework is not an irrelevant bit of gilt round the edges of the narrative but rather a device that Coleridge uses to establish its meaning and direction.

(b) Duration of events

If you were asked to condense the whole story of the Ancient Mariner into a single line, I suppose you might say that it is a poem about a man who shoots an albatross. Coleridge expands this single line into 625, and yet the shooting of the albatross still only takes one of them, and the account of the motivation for this crucial act takes no space at all. That economy clears room in the text for the development of Coleridge's real interest: the unleashing of his imagination as it drives with the ship through icebergs and storms to the terror of the silent sea with its 'slimy things' and psyche-wrenching nightmares. It is almost as though Coleridge, having glimpsed the oceans of consciousness in 'The Eolian Harp' before Sara pulled him back, had now dived right down into its subconscious depths to plunge through all its guilts and fears, searching for truths in sunken caverns as far away as possible from the vacuous good cheer of the wedding-feast. It is that exploration that fills the poem and makes it one of the great triumphs of Romantic literature, a place where the imagination is given full scope to probe the inner self with its silent screams, its hopeless loneliness, its fierce determination to voyage on. All of that is managed through a series of potent symbols: the albatross and the crossbow, the fog and the mist, the bloody sun and the copper sky, the water-snakes and the Nightmare Life-in-Death 'Who thicks man's blood with cold' form a bewildering host that the poet conjures up and trails across the reader's disturbed vision.

(c)   Frequency of events

I say 'disturbed vision'. The thing I find most disturbing, even frustrating, about the poem is the frequency with which the Mariner seems to be about to be released from his cycle of guilt and punishment only to collapse back into it again. The first such moment occurs at the beginning of part II, when the other mariners, having called the shooting of the albatross 'a hellish thing', reverse their stance and forgive him, saying ''Twas right . . . such birds to slay'. The second is in part III, when the Mariner earns the gratitude of the parched crew by biting his own arm to suck the blood, thus enabling him to hail a passing ship. Or there is the moment in part IV when he blesses the water-snakes, the albatross falls from his neck and the prose gloss assures us that 'The spell begins to break'. Again, at the end of part IV, the Mariner hopes that the hermit will be able to 'shrieve my soul' and 'wash away / The Albatross's blood'. But every time these moments of promise come and go and nothing seems to change. The torments resume, 'That agony returns' (l. 583), and the Mariner is pushed back again into his isolating torture. The cycle, it seems, can never be broken, and the poem's very structure re-creates the grip of unpurgeable guilt.

(d)   Point of view

Except for the first five and last two stanzas, which are controlled by an anonymous and self-effacing narrator, it is the Mariner who tells his own story, and at one point he explains why he does so:

> I pass, like night, from land to land;
> I have strange power of speech;
> That moment that his face I see,
> I know the man that must hear me:
> To him my tale I teach.
>   (ll. 586–90)

A man convinced of his 'strange power of speech' and with a compulsion to deliver his message: it is not surprising that many readers, starting indeed with Coleridge himself, have identified the Mariner with Coleridge. Both had discovered wild, strange truths away from the beaten paths of their contemporaries, and both struggled to make others see them, whether by accosting wedding-guests or by berating audiences from platforms in Bristol. It is in this way that the Ancient Mariner has become the type of the Romantic poet, haunted by his sight of the blood and the whirlpools, the corpses and the drought of the world, and striving to convey all of that to the members of the privileged class as they move blithely past to feast and sing in garden bowers. The poet–Mariner is not guaranteed a respectful audience: in the new age of war and revolution, oppression and revolt, he has to fight for a hearing, stand out against easy dismissal as a grey-beard loon who does not belong with decent people going about their decent business. 'The Rime of the Ancient Mariner' is more a poem about the problems of the artist in the Western world than about the inadvisability of shooting albatrosses.

2   Choose a couple of passages and read them closely to make your impression of the poem more specific

We can achieve greater specificity if we look at one of the most frightening episodes in the work, the moment in part III when the ghostly ship carrying Death and Life-in-Death draws alongside:

> Are those *her* ribs through which the Sun
> Did peer, as through a grate?
> And is that Woman all her crew?
> Is that a DEATH? and are there two?
> Is DEATH that woman's mate?

> *Her* lips were red, *her* looks were free,
> Her locks were yellow as gold:
> Her skin was as white as leprosy,
> The Night-mare LIFE-IN-DEATH was she,
> Who thicks man's blood with cold.

> The naked hulk alongside came,
> And the twain were casting dice;

'The game is done! I've won! I've won!'
Quoth she, and whistles thrice.
(ll. 185–98)

What strikes me first about this passage, and it is typical of the whole
poem, is the convincing clarity of detail. It starts with the precise image
of the sun shining through the ship's ribs like the bars of a grate and
follows with a series of direct observations: there are two people in the
ship, they are playing dice, the woman's lips are red, hair yellow, skin
white, and she ends by whistling exactly three times.

And yet, for all that tight precision, these fourteen lines are
simultaneously sinisterly imprecise. There are five questions in the
first stanza, the answers to which we can only guess at because they are
never directly given. And then there is the problem of the meaning
of the details which the passage supplies. Is it significant, for example,
that the woman whistles thrice rather than, say, once or twenty-
seven times? Does the red–yellow–white combination in the second
stanze have a particular symbolic resonance and if so what is it?
And who, anyway, is this Life-in-Death figure? If her victory is as important as it seems at this moment, why do we never hear of her again in
the remaining four hundred and more lines of the ballad? The poem
seems to be terrifyingly vivid and terrifyingly vague at one and the same
time.

The key to all of this seems to me to lie in the sub-title that Coleridge
used for the 1800 edition of the *Lyrical Ballads* but dropped after 1805:
'A Poet's Reverie'. 'The Rime of the Ancient Mariner' works as powerfully as it does because It so successfully mimics the dream process,
which has the capacity to unnerve us precisely because the accuracy of
its detail makes it so believable and also because it is so distressingly
incomprehensible, illogical, full of figures who appear and disappear
without rhyme or reason.

The next passage that I think repays a closer look comes at the end
of the narrative. These are the Mariner's last words as he sums up and
responds to his experience before leaving the poet to deliver the final
two stanzas:

O Wedding-Guest! this soul hath been
Alone on a wide wide sea:
So lonely 'twas, that God himself
Scarce seeméd there to be.

O sweeter than the marriage-feast,
'Tis sweeter far to me,
To walk together to the kirk
With a goodly company! –

To walk together to the kirk,
And all together pray,   .
While each to his great Father bends,
Old men, and babes, and loving friends
And youths and maidens gay!

Farewell, farewell! but this I tell
To thee, thou Wedding-Guest!
He prayeth well, who loveth well
Both man and bird and beast.

He prayeth best, who loveth best
All things both great and small;
For the dear God who loveth us,
He made and loveth all.
                    (ll. 597–617)

The first stanza here, with its *alone* / *lonely* echo, recalls one of the
moments of deepest despair in the poem:

Alone, alone, all, all alone,
Alone on a wide wide sea!
And never a saint took pity on
My soul in agony.
                    (ll. 232–5)

It reminds us that much of the strength of the narrative has been in its
re-creation of the horrors of isolation, the sense of being quite alone in
an irrational universe. Against that primary terror the ballad now sets
an overarching emphasis on the Christian community as a saving alternative. There is the triple repetition of 'together' in the second and third
stanzas, and there is in the second the reference to the church-going
'goodly company' whose wide and comforting membership is specified
at the end of the third. What holds the community together is love,
and the Mariner departs with, in the last two stanzas, a childlike declaration of Christian faith, insisted on by the reiteration of 'loveth' (used
four times).

The problem at this point for many readers is that the conclusion somehow does not fit the poem. By the kind of orthodox Christianity that the Mariner hails, most of the experience in the poem would be rejected as heretical delusion: there are no such things as Polar Spirits; there is no such creature as Life-in-Death who dices for our souls; dead bodies cannot get up to work a ship; and, anyway, shooting a bird is not a sin. Moreover, the deliberately infantile language of these closing lines does not seem to meet in any way the complex adult traumas that the poem describes – for example, the agitated fear of female sexuality that arguably lies behind the Mariner's tale of the deadly red-lipped woman who wins his soul. No wonder the Wedding-Guest at the end is not moved to join the Christian community and its feast, but instead turns away from them to his own brooding introversion.

What seems to me to happen here is a more forceful and extended version of what we saw happening at the finish of 'The Eolian Harp'. In the body of both poems Coleridge the young radical pursues sensuous and psychological experiences to their extremes, touching their soft delights and sounding their alien panic. And then at the end of both poems the discourse shifts and Coleridge the crypto-conservative tries to repress and explain away those dizzying voyages with a flat insistence on simple versions of traditional Christian philosophy. The greatness of 'The Rime of the Ancient Mariner' is that it sees almost in spite of itself that there are more things in heaven and earth than are dreamt of in that philosophy.

3 Sum up your impressions of the poem as a whole

What I think we have seen at work in 'The Rime of the Ancient Mariner' are the two sides of Coleridge briefly sketched at the start of this chapter. First there is the disaffected intellectual, convinced that the narrow rationalism that formed part of the dominant ideology of the late eighteenth century offered an inadequate account of human life and so using his imagination to explore canyons of the mind beyond the reach of that ideology. The poem plunges away from the well-trodden road that leads to the bridegroom's feast. Instead it surges off into regions unexplored by the then-undiscovered science of psychology with a series of intuitive insights into the nature of sexual dread, the grip of a guilt that will not be assuaged or the paradoxically vivid vagueness that is the essence of nightmare. It is in this sense that 'The Rime of the Ancient Mariner' stands with other great radical documents of the

1790s such as Tom Paine's *Rights of Man* and Mary Wollstonecraft's *A Vindication of the Rights of Woman*. All are texts in which we can see humanity taking a leap out of the stagnant swamps of the past and beginning to hack out the paths of the future.

But the future is a lonely, uncharted country, and the poem, while breaking away from the shallow conviviality of the feast at the start, is desperate for the warm companionship that it evokes at the end. And it is then that the other side of Coleridge takes over. The vicar's son who in the year that he wrote the poem decided to snap 'my squeaking baby-trumpet of sedition' and become 'a good man and a Christian' dictates the conclusion of the text. He pitches a simple, even simplistic, version of Christianity against the complex truths that the bulk of the ballad has searched. We are left, I think, sadder and wiser in more ways than one in that final stanza.

IV

Coleridge did not publish 'Kubla Khan' until 1816, although in his note that accompanies the poem he places its composition in the summer of 1797. But in a manuscript copy of the poem he gives the date as 'the fall of the year, 1797', which puts it in the same season that he began writing 'The Rime of the Ancient Mariner'. The two poems share some of the same concerns, as a closer look will show.

The first question we need to face before taking that closer look is to decide whether 'Kubla Khan' is a lyric or narrative poem. Which is the most appropriate of the two methods we have used so far in this book to deploy here in order to read the work with understanding? The answer is that neither method will do on its own, because the poem is both lyric and narrative at one and the same time. It begins, after all, like a story: a narrator introduces Kubla Khan and his decree ordering the construction of a 'stately pleasure-dome', and the text goes on to describe the dome and its setting in 'twice five miles of fertile ground'. But at line 37 the narrative stops and a lyric begins in which the poet through the lyric 'I' explains first that he has somehow lost the inspiration needed to complete the tale and secondly speculates about the results that would follow if only he were capable of recapturing that 'music'. In fracturing the forms of lyric and narrative, binding their pieces together into one text and then publishing the result with the tantalising sub-title 'A Vision in a Dream. A Fragment', Coleridge manifests one more aspect of the Romantic revolt against literary decorum and tradition.

> In Xanadu did Kubla Khan
> A stately pleasure-dome decree:
> Where Alph, the sacred river, ran
> Through caverns measureless to man
>   Down to a sunless sea.   5
> So twice five miles of fertile ground
> With walls and towers were girdled round:
> And there were gardens bright with sinuous rills,
> Where blossomed many an incense-bearing tree;
> And here were forests ancient as the hills,   10
> Enfolding sunny spots of greenery.
>
> But oh! that deep romantic cavern which slanted
> Down the green hill athwart a cedarn cover!
> A savage place! as holy and enchanted
> As e'er beneath a waning moon was haunted   15
> By woman wailing for her demon-lover!
> And from this chasm, with ceaseless turmoil seething,
> As if this earth in fast thick pants were breathing,
> A mighty fountain momently was forced:
> Amid whose swift half-intermitted burst   20
> Huge fragments vaulted like rebounding hail,
> Or chaffy grain beneath the thresher's flail:
> And 'mid these dancing rocks at once and ever
> It flung up momently the sacred river.
> Five miles meandering with a mazy motion   25
> Through wood and dale the sacred river ran,
> Then reached the caverns measureless to man,
> And sank in tumult to a lifeless ocean:
> And 'mid this tumult Kubla heard from far
> Ancestral voices prophesying war!   30
>   The shadow of the dome of pleasure
>   Floated midway on the waves;
>   Where was heard the mingled measure
>   From the fountain and the caves.
> It was a miracle of rare device,   35
> A sunny pleasure-dome with caves of ice!

> A damsel with a dulcimer
> In a vision once I saw:
> It was an Abyssinian maid
> And on her dulcimer she played,   40
> Singing of Mount Abora.
> Could I revive within me
> Her symphony and song,
> To such a deep delight 'twould win me,
> That with music loud and long,   45
> I would build that dome in air,
> That sunny dome! those caves of ice!
> And all who heard should see them there,
> And all should cry, Beware! Beware!
> His flashing eyes, his floating hair!   50
> Weave a circle round him thrice,
> And close your eyes with holy dread,
> For he on honey-dew hath fed,
> And drunk the milk of Paradise.

It would be a mistake, I think, to take the tiny splinter of narrative that we do have and try to split it even further with the dissection method we have used so far for narrative analysis. Of the four main elements of that analysis – order of events, duration of events, frequency of events and point of view – the only really helpful one here is the first. Thus, the poem opens with a suggestion of formal, controlled making. Some sort of ruler, Kubla Khan, decrees the construction of a 'stately pleasure-dome' beside a 'sacred river'. The area is precisely measured ('twice five miles') and contained or 'girdled round' with 'walls and towers'. The result sounds neat and well-ordered with its 'sinuous rills', blossoming trees and 'spots of greenery'.

But this description is followed, as most readers note, with a sharp shift of tone, signalled by the new paragraph and the exclamatory 'But oh!' in line 12. Neat control gives way to exhilarating chaos, as a glance through the vocabulary of the central section illustrates: *chasm, savage, haunted, wailing, demon, ceaseless turmoil seething, fast, forced, burst, fragments, rebounding hail, flail, dancing rocks, flung up, mazy, tumult.* Chaos culminates in line 30 with 'Ancestral voices prophesying war!' For some readers, what comes across here is a sense of contradiction between a human capacity for, on the one hand, calm and rational ordering and control of nature, exemplified in the first eleven lines, and, on the other, the incoherent collapse of all that in passion, war or sexual abandon (suggested by the demon-lover, thick breathing and orgasmic fountain of lines 16–20). But the narrative is broken off before we can determine whether such a reading is legitimate interpretation or wrong-headed speculation. In line 37 we meet 'A damsel with a dulcimer' and appear to have been dropped into a completely different poem.

These last eighteen lines exhibit the sort of lyric structure that we have come across several times already in this book. The main idea is as usual expressed in the form of a fracturing tension. There is massive aspiration, evidenced by the five excited exclamation marks and the quasi-divine status that the poet imagines for himself in the final lines. But undermining and cancelling that is the unavoidable feeling of failure: the work declares itself a fragment, the story stays untold. Just as Wordsworth forged the major achievement of *The Prelude* out of his inability to write *The Recluse*, so Coleridge salvaged out of the wreck of Kubla Khan's tale one of the most celebrated Romantic poems.

If we step back at this point and try to sum up our impressions of the poem as a whole, we can I think see Coleridge working with a structure of ideas parallel to that we have already noted in 'The Rime of the Ancient Mariner', the poem he was writing at the same time. Both are arguably concerned with the artist's problems in finding an audience in an era of violent transition. On the one hand, the Mariner tells his tale successfully but is an outsider, compelled to obtain a solitary listener almost by force. On the other, the 'Kubla Khan' poet dreams about the kind of adoring followers he might win if only he could complete his project. Both, then, are cut off from a wider public and both accordingly present inward-looking visions, texts whose power derives from wild and disparate symbols assembled to suggest inner consciousness with its contradictions, guilts, reveries and obsessions. We can then see the poet figure at the end of 'Kubla Khan', viewed by 'all who heard . . . with holy dread', as a leap of fantasy, an attempt to fabricate an exalted status for the artist, to validate and privilege a mode of imaginative expression that the new social order seems to marginalise with contempt as the outpourings of grey-beard loons.

Coleridge's views on imagination and its operations are frequently offered as his major contribution to English Romanticism. You can trace his theory of imagination in the classic statement in *Biographia Literaria*, chapter 13, that he published in 1817. But before you do that it seems to me important to ask why Coleridge privileges imagination at this time rather than, say, rational judgement or any other faculty. In the same letter to his brother George that I have quoted before in which he claims that he has 'snapped my squeaking baby-trumpet of sedition' and wishes to become 'a good man and a Christian', Coleridge goes on to say:

> And feeling this, my brother! I have for some time past withdrawn myself totally from the consideration of *immediate causes*, which are infinitely complex and uncertain, to muse on fundamental and general causes. . . . I devote myself to such works as encroach not on the anti-social passions – in poetry, to elevate the imagination and set the affections in right tune by the beauty of the inanimate impregnated as 'with a living soul by the presence of life.

In this crucial April 1798 statement we can see Coleridge beginning to outline the terms of a counter-revolution in literature. The poet– Mariner paddles back towards the mainstream and renounces 'sedition', 'anti-social passions' and the analysis of *'immediate causes'* in favour of a more 'general' approach, in particular a poetry that seeks 'to elevate the imagination'.

The problem is that, as he moves his poetry in that direction, it ceases to have anything to say. As he loses contact with the awkward and the socially contentious, his poetry dries up just as surely as the 'Kubla Khan' narrative falters to a halt. Although Coleridge lived for another thirty-six years after 1798, his poetic output dwindled away to nothingness, and he never again reached the disturbing greatness of the work he produced in his years of anguished and contradictory political transition at the end of the eighteenth century. The demands of respectability which we saw blocking the spontaneous flow of 'The Eolian Harp' in the end dammed up Coleridge's poetic genius altogether. The outsider whose jolting visions formed 'The Rime of the Ancient Mariner' lost sight of those visions as he elbowed to join the other guests at the wedding-feast.

The extent to which Coleridge's career as a poet was also destroyed by his opium addiction is now widely accepted. Laudanum, a tincture of opium in alcohol, was then easily available as a pain-killer and he was prescribed substantial doses of it during a bad bout of rheumatic fever he went through while still at school. By 1801 his addiction appears to have been complete, and from 1816 till his death in 1834 he lived with Dr James Gillman, a Highgate surgeon, who helped Coleridge control if not cure his habit. He continued to write and produced volumes of lectures, literary criticism and autobiography. But opium destroyed the capacity for fierce and sustained concentration which was the essence of his poetic process. In one of the last poems he ever wrote, 'Love's Apparition and Evanishment', he imagines himself as 'a lone

Arab', left behind by the caravan of life in 'gradual self-decay' and 'vacant mood'.

Yet it remains a question how far Coleridge's self-destructive slide into opium addiction was his own tragic strategy for suppressing his sense of self-betrayal, as the young radical who bravely confronted the injustices of his age in the early 1790s retreated towards comfortable conservatism by the end of the decade. That perhaps sounds like easy and unverifiable hindsight, but it is worth remembering that it is an analysis first offered by William Hazlitt, Coleridge's friend and the most perceptive of Romantic critics. In *The Spirit of the Age*, first published in 1825, Hazlitt wrote:

> he hailed the rising orb of liberty, since quenched in darkness and in blood, and had kindled his affections at the blaze of the French Revolution, and sang for joy when the towers of the Bastille and the proud places of the insolent and the oppressor fell, and would have floated his bark, freighted with fondest fancies, across the Atlantic wave with Southey and others to seek for peace and freedom. . . .
>
> Alas! 'Frailty, thy name is *Genius!*' – What is become of all this mighty heap of hope, of thought, of learning, and humanity? It has ended in swallowing doses of oblivion and in writing paragraphs in *The Courier* [an evening newspaper]. Such, and so little is the mind of man! . . . Such is the fate of genius in an age, when in the unequal conquest with sovereign wrong, every man is ground to powder who is not either a born slave, or who does not willingly and at once offer up the yearnings of humanity and the dictates of reason as a welcome sacrifice to besotted prejudice and loathsome power.

Notice Hazlitt's analysis of and grief at Coleridge's decline – but notice too Hazlitt's sharp sense of those political struggles that inform Romantic poetry, including the poetry of Keats, the subject of the next chapter.

6

ANALYSING A KEATS POEM

I

JOHN KEATS was born in north London on 31 October 1795 at the Swan and Hoop livery stables. His mother was the daughter of the owner of the stables and his father looked after the horses. His family was broken up first when his father was killed in a riding accident in 1804 and then when his mother died of tuberculosis in 1810. In 1811 his guardian decided to apprentice the sixteen-year-old boy to Thomas Hammond, an apothecary–surgeon, a trade with none of the status that attaches to the medical profession today. Keats worked steadily at his apprenticeship till he received his Apothecaries' Certificate in 1816, but he never practised because by that time his pulsing ambition was to be a writer. His first volume, *Poems*, was published in 1817, and *Endymion* followed in 1818. In 1819 he wrote all three of the poems we shall be looking at in the rest of this chapter.

I have begun with this bald paragraph of facts and dates for two reasons: first, because it helps to contextualise Keats, so that his poems do not come at you from a confusing void but are rooted in an identifiable human being; and, second, because those facts and dates point to the gap we have suddenly crossed from the last four chapters. We have moved on a full generation. When Keats was born in 1795, Blake was thirty-seven, Wordsworth was twenty-five and Coleridge twenty-three. During that generation the world, simply, had changed, with the result that much of the historical framework we have used so far in this book no longer fits.

Take, for example, the question of France. We have seen that the

French Revolution of 1789 and Britain's war (from 1793) against the new French state were wrenchingly formative experiences for such men as Blake, Wordsworth and Coleridge, pushing them towards the angry margins of their own society. But over the years the nature of the French war mutated. Events such as Napoleon's coup in 1799 and his coronation as Emperor in 1804 meant that France was no longer a clear rallying point for liberal and democratic hopes. Napoleon was defeated in 1815, before Keats had published anything, so that his brief career as a poet is confined to the years after the war that had so disturbed the first generation of Romantic writers.

They were years when British society was as close to revolution as it had ever been since the civil wars of the seventeenth century; when 300,000 soldiers and sailors were released from the army and navy to look for jobs that did not exist; when 100,000 people demonstrating for Parliamentary reform near Manchester in 1819 were attacked by the yeomanry, leaving eleven dead. They were years when radical journalists such as William Hone, Richard Carlile and Leigh Hunt were imprisoned; when the Government strove to hold down society by force and by the fiercely repressive legislation of 1817 and 1819. In 'Sonnet: England in 1819' Shelley scoffed at 'An old, mad, blind, despised and dying king' – George III – presiding over 'A people starved and stabbed in the untilled field' together with

Rulers who neither see, nor feel, nor know,
But leech-like to their fainting country cling.

When one of those rulers, the Foreign Secretary Castlereagh, committed suicide in 1822, people showed up at his funeral to cheer, whilst in 1817 they had pelted the Prince Regent at the state opening of Parliament.

What lies behind this brutal bitterness is the sharper class division in British society, deepened by the Industrial Revolution and then widened by the profits and losses springing from the twenty-two year war with France. In that tense and fractured era every detail of life became overtly politicised and every choice in life from the company you kept to the journals you read involved taking sides.

Keats was too intensely brave to shrink from the challenge of these times. The very first poem in his first volume, *Poems* (1817), was dedicated to Leigh Hunt. Hunt was the editor of *The Examiner*, a liberal weekly, and a man who had recently spent two years in prison for his paper's attacks on the Prince Regent. Another sonnet in the same volume, titled 'Written on the Day that Mr Leigh Hunt Left Prison', scorned the 'wretched crew' who had locked him up for 'showing truth to flatter'd state'. The Tory reviews that disciplined and organised literary taste at the time picked up the message. John Lockhart, a ferocious reactionary, responded to Keats's next volume, *Endymion*, in *Blackwood's Edinburgh Magazine* for August 1818 and headlined his piece 'Cockney School of Poetry'. The sneer of snobbery in that phrase runs right through the review, whether it is in the revealing protest that an apothecary's apprentice such as Keats should join the 'many farm-servants and unmarried ladies' and even 'our very footmen' who presume to literary production in 'this mad age', or in the disdainful complaint aimed at those 'without learning enough to distinguish between the written language of Englishmen and the spoken jargon of Cockneys'. The Tory MP John Wilson Croker reinforced the attack in the September 1818 *Quarterly Review*, jeering at 'Cockney poetry; which may be defined to consist of the most incongruous ideas in the most uncouth language'.

In short, the British establishment hated 'Johnny Keats' (Lockhart's term) and all his works. They hated him because he was a Cockney and a man who did not go to university. They hated him because of his ordinary origins and because he had worked as an apprentice. Above all they hated him because from the very start of his brief career he championed radical writers and radical ideas. (As Lockhart put it, 'their bantling has already learned to lisp sedition'.) And so they tried to shut him up, Lockhart concluding his review with the advice, 'It is a better and wiser thing to be a starved apothecary than a starved poet.' Remember these things when you read Keats and they will help you to see him clearly through the mists of sentimental criticism that have sometimes clung to him since his death, mists which can distort him and turn him into a dim, watery figure warbling over-sensitive lyrics at a safe distance from vulgar reality. The British ruling class knew better than that and could recognise a dangerous enemy when it saw one. Otherwise one of its anonymous spokesmen would not have bothered to pontificate in the *Literary Critic* on 8 December 1821, after Keats's death, calling him 'a foolish young man', a 'radically presumptuous profligate' and author of 'very indecent poetry'. Let us have a good look at some of that very indecent poetry.

II

Leigh Hunt was the first to publish Keats's 'La Belle Dame sans Merci', not in *The Examiner* but in another periodical he edited, *The Indicator*, on 10 May 1820. Nowadays a better-known and slightly different version of the poem is the one Keats dated 21 April 1819 and included in a letter to his younger brother George and his wife Georgiana. At forty-eight lines, it is a very much briefer narrative poem than any of those we have looked at in earlier chapters, but the method for narrative analysis that we have used before will still work in this case.

I

O, what can ail thee, knight-at-arms,
    Alone and palely loitering?
The sedge has wither'd from the lake,
    And no birds sing.

II

O, what can ail thee, knight-at-arms,   5
    So haggard and so woe-begone?
The squirrel's granary is full,
    And the harvest's done.

III

I see a lilly on thy brow,
    With anguish moist and fever dew;   10
And on thy cheeks a fading rose
    Fast withereth too.

IV

I met a lady in the meads,
    Full beautiful – a faery's child,
Her hair was long, her foot was light,   15
    And her eyes were wild.

V

I made a garland for her head,
    And bracelets too, and fragrant zone;
She look'd at me as she did love,
    And made sweet moan.   20

VI

I set her on my pacing steed,
    And nothing else saw all day long;
For sidelong would she bend, and sing
    A faery's song.

VII

She found me roots of relish sweet,   25
    And honey wild, and manna dew,
And sure in language strange she said –
    'I love thee true'.

VIII

She took me to her elfin grot,
    And there she wept and sigh'd full sore,   30
And there I shut her wild wild eyes
    With kisses four.

IX

And there she lulled me asleep
    And there I dream'd – Ah! woe betide!
The latest dream I ever dream'd   35
    On the cold hill side.

X

I saw pale kings and princes too,
    Pale warriors, death-pale were they all;
They cried – 'La Belle Dame sans Merci
    Hath thee in thrall!'   40

XI

I saw their starved lips in the gloam,
    With horrid warning gaped wide,
And I awoke and found me here,
    On the cold hill's side.

XII

And this is why I sojourn here   45
    Alone and palely loitering,
Though the sedge has wither'd from the lake,
    And no birds sing.

I   Read the poem and try to work out the way the story is patterned

(a)   Order of events

I think the most obvious thing about the ordering of this poem is that
it presents the same pattern as 'The Rime of the Ancient Mariner' in

that in both texts we know the broad outcome of the story before we are even told it. So, here, we know after six lines that the knight is 'alone and palely loitering', 'haggard' and 'woe-begone'. That desolate sense of failure is reinforced by the seasonal references in the first three stanzas: the sedge (a kind of grass that grows in marshy areas) has withered, the birds have gone, the harvest is done and so on. The energy and sap of life has clearly moved on and left the knight behind, a dilapidated relic. All of this means that when the knight takes over the poem at line 13 and begins to tell the story of love, the reader knows from the start that it is doomed, for all its garlands, songs, kisses and dreams. We are distanced from the illusions of love that are described in the central five stanzas because the opening has warned us that they are false. We do not believe them; they simply hurt, and hurt all the more for their apparent sweetness.

(b)   Duration of events

After three stanzas in which an anonymous figure sets the mood and asks the knight a series of questions, the knight himself speaks and narrates the final nine stanzas. These in turn can be further subdivided. For five stanzas, from line 13 to line 32, he describes his infatuation and overloads the poem with conventional romantic language: *Full beautiful, faery's child, bracelets, sweet moan, faery's song, honey, elfin grot, sigh'd, wild wild eyes, kisses four*. And then suddenly all of that sensuality is shunted aside by four concluding stanzas of nightmare: *woe betide!, cold, death-pale, in thrall, starved lips, gloam, horrid warning gaped wide*, and so on. A lot of the strange power of the poem comes from the contradictory tension generated by juxtaposing these two roughly equal blocks of emotional extremes: the silkiest of erotic fantasies is pushed tight up against gross Gothic horror and then the poem stops. The reader is pulled hard in two opposite directions and then, like the knight, simply abandoned.

(c)   Frequency of events

A noticeable feature of the text is the frequency with which words, phrases, lines and rhythm patterns are repeated. The last three lines of the poem, for example, rerun the end of the first stanza almost exactly. What this suggests to me is a sense of deadlocked frustration, a complete absence of progress. Eleven stanzas and a whole story on from the start and we seem to get nowhere at all, the opening statement being repeated with no meaningful variation or advance. The poem, like the knight, is stuck in a groove from which it cannot escape.

Some readers have suggested that the unusual rhythm pattern repeated in each stanza increases this sense of frustration. The normal ballad metre, on which this text is based, alternates four-beat and three-beat lines. Here, the last line of each stanza is a foot short and only has two beats. It is as though there were a bit missing: at the end of each stanza the voice feels for part of a line that is not there and the momentum of the narrative is lost. You may feel that this is a rather fanciful explanation. But the fact is that Keats does break from normal ballad metre and repeats the break twelve times in twelve stanzas. The aborted rhythm seems to echo, at the level of the poem's form, the knight's sexual block which is the poem's subject. It is not easy to think of any other satisfactory interpretation of this conscious stylistic oddity.

(d)   Point of view

'La Belle Dame sans Merci' is cast in dialogue form, with repeated questions from an unnamed observer provoking the knight's narration. This is a traditional structure that you will find in many ballads, and we have already seen something similar at the beginning of 'The Rime of the Ancient Mariner'. The reason Keats uses it here is to set up the effect we have already described – namely, the observer's sketch of the scene and of the knight makes the latter's sour loss plain even before he opens his mouth, and casts a gloom forward over the knight's bright opening words. He recounts his engrossing happiness before his plunge into lonely despair, but the reader is glumly forewarned from the start and watches the knight's enchantment with mounting anticipation of catastrophe.

2   Choose a couple of passages and read them closely to make your impression of the poem more specific

This narrative poem is fairly short and so a single passage will suffice for closer examination. I have chosen the tenth stanza because it is the moment when the story's secret is revealed and we learn the reason for the knight's distress:

> I saw pale kings and princes too,
>   Pale warriors, death-pale were they all;

> They cried – 'La Belle Dame sans Merci
> Hath thee in thrall!'

'La Belle Dame sans Merci' means 'the beautiful lady without pity'. Why does Keats put it in French? It is in fact the title of a work by the French poet Alain Chartier, written in 1424, but the title is all that Keats takes from Chartier's text. What the French does is to make the subject foreign; it gives the woman an air of mystery that she would have lacked if he had called her, say, Jane Cox or Fanny Brawne – real women that Keats knew at the time. The name contributes to the general estrangement that is at work in this stanza and elsewhere in the poem. The kings, princes and warriors, the knight-at-arms himself and the faery's child, the meads and the pacing steed are all part of the 'language strange' (l. 27) of the ballad which distances it far from early-nineteenth-century Hampstead, where Keats was living when he wrote it. The medieval remoteness allows him to stretch his material, to magnify the delights and the terrors of love and sexuality, in ways that would have been impossible without absurdity were he pinned to the narrow realities of lower-middle-class London in April 1819. It means that sexual attraction and sexual frustration can be explored with an intensity which generations of readers since have found disturbingly moving.

3   Sum up your impressions of the poem as a whole

'La Belle Dame sans Merci' opens with a scene of decay from the withered sedge in the first stanza and links that landscape by means of the 'fading rose' in the third stanza with the forlorn knight who inhabits it. What follows is a tale of extremes, extremes of sexual arousal and sexual denial, a ballad that veers from the kisses and the fragrance and the sweet moans of the central section to the death-pale figures, the starved lips and the cold hill side of the conclusion.

It seems to me a mistake to tidy the poem away by explaining it simply in terms of Keats's grief at the death of his brother Tom the previous December or his tangled feelings for Fanny Brawne, to whom he became provisionally engaged at about this time. After all, when Keats wanted to write poems about Tom or Fanny, he did so directly, several times, without recourse to medieval French ladies. But what the love and the loss of those months did do to Keats was to enable him to make a poem about the intensity of desire and the intensity of its defeat. In the same April letter to George and Georgiana in which he transcribed 'La Belle Dame sans Merci' he went on to argue:

> The common cognomen of this world among the misguided and super-
> stitious is 'a vale of tears' from which we are to be redeemed by a certain
> arbitrary interposition of God and taken to Heaven – What a little cir-
> cumscribed straightened notion! Call the world if you please 'The vale of
> Soul-making'. Then you will find out the use of the world.

Keats had been through his own 'vale of Soul-making' in the months before he wrote 'La Belle Dame sans Merci'. The result was a poem which begins as a presentation of a certain kind of male sexuality involving piercing need for a woman cut across and blocked by fear of women. But it then grows beyond that into a great statement about love and rejection and confronting that rejection without pious props or trite morals as relief. No wonder the bigot who wrote for the *Literary Critic* found Keats's poetry 'very indecent'.

III

In the same month that Keats wrote 'La Belle Dame sans Merci' he also wrote 'Ode to Psyche', and in the next month, May 1819, he followed that with four more odes, 'Ode to a Nightingale', 'Ode on a Grecian Urn', 'Ode on Melancholy' and 'Ode on Indolence', to complete the most wondrously creative weeks of his short life. His choice of the ode as the form through which to express that creativity is worth examining for a moment.

The term 'ode' is derived from a Greek word meaning 'song' and during ancient times denoted one of several varieties of lyric. The form was used in English poetry from the sixteenth century onwards and by Keats's day meant an elaborate lyric usually addressed to a person, object or quality that the poet revered. The ode was a chance to celebrate and explore the nature of the admired subject and the moods it evoked in the contemplating poet.

We have already seen that at this period Keats was under attack from the political and literary establishment, and the quotation from the 21 April 1819 letter in the last section shows his impatience with conventional religious beliefs. The ode, at this difficult juncture in his life, gave him the opportunity to research his own experience for sources of value, support and consolation alternative to those inscribed in the dominant

religious and political systems of the day. We can see what he made of
that opportunity if we take one of the May odes, 'Ode to a Nightingale', and work through it with the method for reading a lyric we have
used in earlier chapters.

I

My heart aches, and a drowsy numbness pains
   My sense, as though of hemlock I had drunk,
Or emptied some dull opiate to the drains
   One minute past, and Lethe-wards had sunk:
'Tis not through envy of thy happy lot,   5
   But being too happy in thine happiness, –
      That thou, light-winged Dryad of the trees,
         In some melodious plot
   Of beechen green, and shadows numberless,
      Singest of summer in full-throated ease.   10

II

O, for a draught of vintage! that hath been
   Cool'd a long age in the deep-delved earth,
Tasting of Flora and the country green,
   Dance, and Provençal song, and sunburnt mirth!
O for a beaker full of the warm South   15
   Full of the true, the blushful Hippocrene,
      With beaded bubbles winking at the brim,
         And purple-stained mouth;
   That I might drink, and leave the world unseen,
      And with thee fade away into the forest dim: 20

III

Fade far away, dissolve, and quite forget
   What thou among the leaves hast never known,
The weariness, the fever, and the fret
   Here, where men sit and hear each other groan;
Where palsy shakes a few, sad, last gray hairs,   25
   Where youth grows pale, and spectre-thin, and dies;
      Where but to think is to be full of sorrow
         And leaden-eyed despairs,
   Where Beauty cannot keep her lustrous eyes,
      Or new Love pine at them beyond to-morrow.   30

IV

Away! away! for I will fly to thee,
   Not charioted by Bacchus and his pards,
But on the viewless wings of Poesy,
   Though the dull brain perplexes and retards:
Already with thee! tender is the night,   35
   And haply the Queen-Moon is on her throne,
      Cluster'd around by all her starry Fays;
         But here there is no light,
   Save what from heaven is with the breezes blown
      Through verdurous glooms and winding mossy ways.   40

V

I cannot see what flowers are at my feet,
   Nor what soft incense hangs upon the boughs,
But, in embalmed darkness, guess each sweet
   Wherewith the seasonable month endows
The grass, the thicket, and the fruit-tree wild;   45
   White hawthorn, and the pastoral eglantine;
      Fast fading violets cover'd up in leaves;
         And mid-May's eldest child,
   The coming musk-rose, full of dewy wine,
      The murmurous haunt of flies on summer eves.   50

VI

Darkling I listen; and, for many a time
   I have been half in love with easeful Death,
Call'd him soft names in many a mused rhyme,
   To take into the air my quiet breath;
Now more than ever seems it rich to die,   55
   To cease upon the midnight with no pain,
      While thou art pouring forth thy soul abroad
         In such an ecstasy!
   Still wouldst thou sing, and I have ears in vain —
      To thy high requiem become a sod.   60

VII

Thou wast not born for death, immortal Bird!
   No hungry generations tread thee down;
The voice I hear this passing night was heard
   In ancient days by emperor and clown:

Perhaps the self-same song that found a path   65
   Through the sad heart of Ruth, when, sick for home,
      She stood in tears amid the alien corn;
         The same that oft-times hath
Charm'd magic casements, opening on the foam
   Of perilous seas, in faery lands forlorn.   70

                        VIII
Forlorn! the very word is like a bell
   To toll me back from thee to my sole self!
Adieu! the fancy cannot cheat so well
   As she is fam'd to do, deceiving elf.
Adieu! adieu! thy plaintive anthem fades   75
   Past the near meadows, over the still stream,
      Up the hill-side; and now 'tis buried deep
         In the next valley-glades:
Was it a vision, or a waking dream?
   Fled is that music: – Do I wake or sleep?   80

I   Look for the main idea or feeling

An idea that occurs several times in this poem is a fantasy of escape. In
the opening lines it is associated with drugs – 'hemlock' or 'some dull
opiate'. In stanza two the vehicle is alcohol, the 'draught of vintage',
that will enable the poet to 'drink, and leave the world unseen'. By
stanza four alcohol is rejected in favour of the 'wings of Poesy', which
will let the poet fly to a realm of imagination even though 'the dull
brain perplexes and retards'. And then in stanza six death itself is
invoked as the ultimate withdrawal from reality, allowing the poet to
'cease upon the midnight with no pain'.

   As well as drugs, alcohol, poetry and death, the nightingale itself is,
of course, the main symbol of escape in the ode, the others being the
means to help the poet break free and 'with thee fade away into the
forest dim'. The bird has a series of qualities that make it an appropriate focus for Keats's dreams of flight: its happiness in stanza one, for
example, its ignorance of human suffering in stanza three, or even its
apparent immortality in stanza seven, so that it seems

   The voice I hear this passing night was heard
      In ancient days by emperor and clown. . . .

But, as we have seen so often in this book, the main ideas in Romantic lyrics are rarely expressed without some tension, and there are at least two powerful elements here that stop the ode from being a simplistic song about coping with life by escaping through drugs. First, the poet is clearly too much in love with life and the sensations it offers to want to drift off into numbness – look, for example, at the sheer sensuous delight that works in every line of stanza two. And, secondly, if the fantasy is to range with genuine freedom it must at some point blunder into words such as 'forlorn', which it does at the end of stanza seven. At once the precious escapist illusion that has been offered in, say, stanza four, with all its exaggerated poeticisms ('Bacchus and his pards', 'the Queen-Moon' and 'all her starry Fays'), falls to pieces. Fantasy can certainly dream of a nightingale that 'Singest of summer in full-throated ease' (l. 10), but the same fantasy, with its mooring in Keats's experience, can also turn that summer song into a 'high requiem' (l. 60) or a 'plaintive anthem' (l. 75). The brain can play games with the world but in the end the world remains and intrudes. So it is that 'Ode to a Nightingale' becomes simultaneously and contradictorily a poem about the need to escape, the delights of escape and the impossibility and futility of escape.

2   Look at the choices and combinations of words that express the main idea or feeling

If we look more closely at the words Keats uses in the poem we can see what it is he is trying to escape from and where he is trying to escape to. Sometimes he wants to flee to a place that is geographically remote, as he conjures up 'the warm South' with its 'Dance, and Provençal song' in stanza two. But above all that place is culturally remote, its persuasions are solidly pagan and worlds away from early-nineteenth-century Anglicanism. Hence the poem is full of references to the beliefs and the gods of ancient Greece and Rome: Lethe, the river whose waters made the drinker forget, and the Dryad, the nymph of the trees, in stanza one; Flora, the Roman goddess of flowers, and Hippocrene, the fountain sacred to the muses in southern Greece, in stanza two; Bacchus, the Roman god of wine, in stanza four. There is too the 'Queen-Moon' and her attendant fairies or 'Fays', also in stanza four, and we are back in 'faery lands' again at the end of stanza seven.

What Keats is running away from is made plain enough in stanza three; it is

The weariness, the fever, and the fret
  Here, where men sit and hear each other groan;
Where palsy shakes a few, sad, last gray hairs,
    Where youth grows pale, and spectre-thin, and dies;
      Where but to think is to be full of sorrow
        And leaden-eyed despairs.

With those truths put with such tough clarity, it is inevitable that the poet's attempt to forget them in the rest of the ode should fail. But, before the failure is faced, Keats's mind wanders erratically through pagan mythology, enticing because utterly remote from 1819. He dallies with Flora and Bacchus, with Dryads and the Queen-Moon, to see if there is sense or consolation to be had in the beliefs that humanity in the past has used to explain and control the world. For all their nostalgic charm and cultural prestige, none of these alternatives work. At the end the poet is left forlorn to confront the facts of life that stanza three baldly lists.

3   Focus on the lines which clinch your sense of the poem's main idea or feeling

How exactly does Keats convey the failure to escape that the poem records? The moment comes at the start of the last stanza:

Forlorn! the very word is like a bell
  To toll me back from thee to my sole self!
Adieu! the fancy cannot cheat so well
  As she is fam'd to do, deceiving elf.

The poet is thrown back on his isolated subjectivity, on 'my sole self', after dreams of breaking out of that subjectivity using, say, alcohol have dissolved. But, as Keats notes in these lines, the main escape vehicle in the poem has not been artificial stimulants but 'the fancy', the fancy that seized on the nightingale and wove around it and its song all the images and desires of the first seven stanzas.

In the last chapter we saw Coleridge privileging the fancy or imagination, offering its processes and its capacities as a kind of conservative consolation in an era of disappointment and defeat. 'Ode to a Nightingale' seems to me to work through that illusion. For seventy lines Keats lets his imagination run wild, cavorting through its own enticing landscapes and creating perhaps the best-known flight of fantasy in all Romantic poetry. And yet, for all that, Keats at the end arrives at a flat axiom: 'the fancy cannot cheat so well/As she is fam'd to do, deceiving elf'. To call the fancy an 'elf' is to make it of a piece with all the other fairies and godlings and what-nots that have filled the ode, pleasant enough but finally no more use than a brick lifebelt when floundering in a world where, for that 'sole self', 'but to think is to be full of sorrow'. Philistine suggestions at this point that maybe Keats needed to cheer himself up a bit forget both the poem's own pervading sense of the delights of life and the poet's own realisation (hinted at in stanza six) that he was dying of tuberculosis and still not twenty-four. The ode is driven by a fierce passion to escape, by a brilliant indulgence in that escape and by a closing insistence that attempts at escape are 'deceiving', a 'cheat'.

4 Sum up your impressions of the poem as a whole

The best way to begin a summary of the 'Ode to a Nightingale' in the context of this chapter is perhaps to link it back to 'La Belle Dame sans Merci', the last poem we looked at and one that Keats wrote the previous month. Both texts present us with beautiful illusions: here, it is a rapid series of escapist visions, culminating in the 'faery lands forlorn' of stanza seven; 'La Belle Dame sans Merci' was about one illusion, 'a faery's child'. Both poems construct their pretty illusions with immense verbal and technical skill and both end by insisting on their desolating failure as delights or as solace.

By the age of twenty-three, of course, most people can cope with the realisation that fairies do not exist without its inducing in them the sense of abandoned despair Keats conveys at the close of both texts. But to say that is to miss Keats's point, which is precisely to suggest that most readily available sources of consolation, from the banality of alcohol through the excitements of 'Poesy' up to the ecstasy of romantic love, *are* little more than fairy stories – powerful, infantile dreams without real substance. Keats in stanza three of 'Ode to a Nightingale' presents the pain of life as seen through the eyes of a dying young man in 1819, marked out as an enemy by an establishment busy organising the world's first industrial economy and not prepared to tolerate the uneasy reservations of Romantic poets. He briefly ransacks mythology in a vain search for a defence or a refuge. He is not even tempted to

dig out childhood's catechism in the way that Coleridge does at the conclusion of 'The Rime of the Ancient Mariner'. But what he constructs
out of his own inability to find a hiding place is a glorious statement
about human desires and aspirations, their infinite reach and capacity,
their nightingale-like speed and fluidity, and yet the absolute impossibility of their realisation in the sort of society that Keats inhabited. It
was a central contradiction facing humanity and the greatest of Keats's
poems centrally explore it.

IV

In the spring (1819) when Keats wrote his series of odes, he gave up
Hyperion, his attempt to write a major narrative poem about revolutionary social change through the medium of Greek mythology. This
legend of the Titans and their overthrow by a new race of gods, the
Olympians, he then set about recasting through the summer of 1819
as a new poem called *The Fall of Hyperion: A Dream*, but by September
it was clear that that text too had faltered to a halt. Keats was fasci-
nated by the processes of and the possibilities for personal and social
progress. But the autumn of 1819 was not an auspicious time to develop
those hopes, and the passage of the notorious Six Acts made the realisation of such hopes even more remote. The historian E.P. Thompson,
in *The Making of the English Working Class* (1968), has described that
moment as follows:

> The Six Acts appear as a codification and extension of the legislation of
> 1795 and 1817. The first Act prohibited drilling and 'military' training: the
> second authorised justices to enter and search houses, without warrants,
> on suspicion of there being arms: the third prohibited meetings exceed-
> ing fifty in number, with certain exceptions (county and parish meetings)
> and additions (designed to suppress Radical lecture-meetings): the fourth
> Act (of great importance in the next twelve years) increased the stamp
> duty on periodical publications, raising their cost to 6d. and above: the
> fifth and sixth Acts were designed to extend and expedite the powers of
> the authorities, especially in actions for seditious libel. . . . Thereafter the
> Government launched upon the most sustained campaign of prosecutions
> in the courts in British history. . . . A major assault had commenced against
> the 'seditious' and 'blasphemous' press. Scores of prosecutions, against
> publishers or newsvendors, had been instituted by the private prosecut-
> ing societies or dealt with by summary jurisdiction.   (p. 768)

In a letter Keats wrote on 18 September 1819 he responded indignantly
to this situation with a passage that intriguingly conducts political
analysis by means of a metaphor of germination and growth:

> the liberal writers of france and england sowed the seed of opposition to
> this Tyranny – and it was swelling in the ground till it burst out in the french
> revolution – That has had an unlucky termination. It put a stop to the rapid
> progress of free sentiments in England; and gave our Court hopes of
> turning back to the despotism of the 16 century. They have made a handle
> of this event in every way to undermine our freedom. They spread a
> horrid superstition against all inovation and improvement – The present
> struggle in England of the people is to destroy this superstition. What has
> rous'd them to do it is their distresses. . . .

The very next day he moved beyond germination and growth to the
next stage, ripeness and decay, and wrote his ode 'To Autumn'. In it he
strove to carry on thinking about the process of evolution and revolution in men and women, in nature and societies, in terms that were
honest but which would not land his publisher in prison. Let us look at
what he has to say.

I

Season of mists and mellow fruitfulness,
    Close bosom-friend of the maturing sun;
Conspiring with him how to load and bless
    With fruit the vines that round the thatch-eves run;
To bend with apples the moss'd cottage-trees,   5
    And fill all fruit with ripeness to the core;
        To swell the gourd, and plump the hazel shells
With a sweet kernel; to set budding more,
    And still more, later flowers for the bees,
    Until they think warm days will never cease,   10
        For Summer has o'er-brimm'd their clammy cells.

II

Who hath not seen thee oft amid thy store?
    Sometimes whoever seeks abroad may find
Thee sitting careless on a granary floor,
    Thy hair soft-lifted by the winnowing wind;   15
Or on a half-reap'd furrow sound asleep,
    Drows'd with the fume of poppies, while thy hook

>   Spares the next swath and all its twined flowers:
> And sometimes like a gleaner thou dost keep
>   Steady thy laden head across a brook;   20
>   Or by a cyder-press, with patient look,
>   Thou watchest the last oozings hours by hours.
>
>   III
> Where are the songs of Spring? Ay, where are they?
>   Think not of them, thou hast thy music too, –
> While barred clouds bloom the soft-dying day,   25
>   And touch the stubble-plains with rosy hue;
> Then in a wailful choir the small gnats mourn
>   Among the river sallows, borne aloft
>   Or sinking as the light wind lives or dies;
> And full-grown lambs loud bleat from hilly bourn;   30
>   Hedge-crickets sing; and now with treble soft
> The red-breast whistles from a garden-croft;
>   And gathering swallows twitter in the skies.

I   Look for the main idea or feeling

Well, obviously this is a poem about autumn, as we might gather from
the title. But why autumn rather than, say, old books or bear-baiting?
And what does Keats actually do with his subject? What does he make
of it?

It seems to me that he centres two aspects of autumn for our attention. In the first lines it is all 'mellow fruitfulness' under the 'maturing
sun', and the opening stanza is packed with apples and gourds, nuts
and flowers, fruit and bees. But, besides being a time of abundance,
autumn is also the season of decay and death, and the last stanza is
by comparison relatively barren as the 'soft-dying day' settles on the
'stubble-plains', the 'gnats mourn' and the swallows prepare to leave.

Yet there is none of the forlorn gloom in the face of the fullness of
life and then its losses that we found at the end of 'La Belle Dame sans
Merci' or 'Ode to a Nightingale'. In the letter, already quoted, that he
wrote the day before composing 'To Autumn', Keats went on to argue:

> The present struggle in England of the people is to destroy this supersti-
> tion. What has rous'd them to do it is their distresses – Perhaps on this
> account the present distresses of this nation are a fortunate thing – tho so
> horrid in their experience.

He is still working at that idea in parallel terms in 'To Autumn'. He has rejected Christianity and so does not look to that for comfort in confronting death and distress, and he has turned away from the relics of pagan belief after his failure that year to complete either *Hyperion* or *The Fall of Hyperion*. Instead, he moves from religion and mythology to actual, lived experience, whether it is the rebellious discontent of England in 1819 or the mists of those autumn days. In those experiences he searches for firmer sources of hope in what he calls in his letter written on 18 September 'the present struggle in England of the people', or what he sees in his ode written on 19 September as the inevitable processes of growth, decay and change. Summer gives way to autumn but beyond autumn there is spring, spring which is alluded to at the start of the last stanza and whose certainty makes the onset of winter acceptable. The poem presents that acceptance and the paradoxical benefits of decay, just as the day before the letter had thought through to the paradoxical benefits of distress. The letter looks at and learns positive lessons from the tyranny of September 1819, and in a similar trajectory the poem observes and wins hope from 'the last oozings' of that autumn.

2   Look at the choices and combinations of words that express the main idea or feeling

We have already seen in this chapter that a lot of the power in Keats's poetry is generated by juxtaposing opposites: the knight's erotic dreams against dire nightmare at the end of 'La Belle Dame sans Merci', or escapist blisses opposed to 'leaden-eyed despairs' in 'Ode to a Nighingale'. Initially it seems as though the same effect is being set up here as Keats works strenuously in the first stanza to create a sense of superabundance: *fruitfulness, maturing, load, bless, fruit, bend, ripeness, swell, plump, sweet, budding, still more, flowers, warm, never cease, Summer, o'er brimm'd* – nearly every word in the first eleven lines adds to an impression of overflowing fertility. The result is that, when Autumn is personified in the second stanza, he/she can afford to be at ease after all the energetic swelling and plumping of the first stanza, whether sitting carelessly in the granary, sleeping on the furrow, holding steady across the brook or passively watching the 'cyder-press'.

But look at the language in the last stanza: *barred clouds, soft-dying, stubble, wailful, mourn, sinking, dies, bleat*. If 'To Autumn' works with a series of buried musical metaphors (see, for example, in this last stanza, *songs, music, choir, sing, treble soft, whistles, twitter*), then the note that is being introduced into the arrangement here is of death and its attendant sorrows. But what follow are not the disruptive dischords of 'La Belle Dame sans Merci' or 'Ode to a Nightingale'. There is no broken despair as at the close of those poems. Instead, the melody holds and the mood of patient, unruffled description is maintained without wavering down to the very last line.

3   Focus on the lines which clinch your sense of the poem's main idea or feeling

Let us look at precisely how Keats keeps that mood going right through to the end:

> Hedge-crickets sing; and now with treble soft
> The red-breast whistles from a garden-croft;
>   And gathering swallows twitter in the skies.

It is very simple material: crickets sing, robins whistle, swallows twitter. Keats straightforwardly describes some of the sights and sounds and colours of autumn in those last three lines as he has done all through the poem. The first stanza is one long sentence, a series of parallel phrases and clauses woven together with five co-ordinating *and*s. The four personifications of the ten-line sentence in stanza two are linked very simply with *or* (twice) and *and*. This piling up of impressions continues right through the last stanza. Again, the ten-line concluding sentence is quite plainly constructed: four *and*s and two *or*s lay out the experiences in an uncomplicated list and there is no attempt at prioritising one or subordinating another. The seasonal process flows steadily on; event succeeds event; Keats watches and records. The 'fruitfulness' of stanza one has been replaced by the 'soft-dying' of stanza three, but the poet remains undistraught, not 'forlorn' as at the end of 'Ode to a Nightingale' and with none of the 'horrid warning' that shakes 'La Belle Dame sans Merci'. He just goes on looking and listening: first the cricket, then the robin, finally the swallows. Death, distress and struggle, all of those terms that stormed and blasted him in 1819, he now takes in his stride, and the ode moves through them all to its close, patiently noting, never flinching, rock-steady.

4   Sum up your impressions of the poem as a whole

'To Autumn', unsurprisingly, is about autumn. It records some of the occurrences of the season, delighting first in its abundance and then easing towards a sense of death and departure in the final stanza. This transition and its contemplation are achieved with a tone of hopeful acceptance rather than the vacant despair of 'La Belle Dame sans Merci' or the comfortless terror of being driven back into 'my sole self' at the end of 'Ode to a Nightingale'. Those poems were about failed illusions; 'To Autumn' roots itself not in illusion but in the painful, unavoidable yet finally bearable experience of the real world and its seasonal flux. That process is not poeticised by the introduction of classical gods, not sanctified by reference to the Christian God. It is there, it is negotiated in the text and confronted without supports in a way that generates its own strengths. Keats faces life as it sinks towards winter, takes lyrical pleasure in its beauty and notes down its incipient decay. It is done with quiet courage, the same sort of courage to struggle in the face of distress that he admired in the people of England the day before he wrote the ode.

In the end, Keats appears to have lived on that courage and nothing else. A year and a half later he died of the tuberculosis that he knew was killing him as he worked on 'To Autumn'. His friend Joseph Severn, who nursed him through his last days, wrote:

> I am broken down from four nights' watching, and no sleep since, and my poor Keats gone. Three days since, the body was opened; the lungs were completely gone. The Doctors could not conceive by what means he had lived these two months.

Johnny Keats, the Cockney from the Swan and Hoop livery stables, died with the bravery he used for living and for writing poetry.

7

WORKING WITH WOMEN'S POETRY

I

IN THE FIRST edition of this book, published in 1988, there was no chapter like this one dealing with poetry written by women during the Romantic period. If there is another edition in a dozen years' time, there will almost certainly be separate chapters about the work of individual women poets. What these changes mark is the revolution going on at present in our understanding of the contribution made by women to the history of English poetry in the late eighteenth and early nineteenth century.

This book is deliberately shaped around the poetry which is readily available in paperback form and which therefore appears on university and school syllabuses. In the late 1980s there was no chapter on women's Romantic poetry because none of it was easily available and so none of it was studied. This situation began to change in 1990 with the publication of Roger Lonsdale's anthology *Eighteenth-Century Women Poets* for Oxford University Press, followed in 1992 by Jennifer Breen's *Women Romantic Poets 1785–1832: An Anthology*, published by Everyman. Several similar collections have since followed (see the Further Reading section at the end of this book.) For the first time in nearly two hundred years, we have easily available samples of the wide variety of work published by women at the same time that Blake, Wordsworth and Keats were writing and as a result that work is beginning to be studied in schools and universities. Anthologies are only a start. I find they often frustrate as much as they stimulate and raise more questions than they answer: for instance, are these two or three poems the best the author wrote? or a random sample? or an eccentric sample? The complete works of one or two poets or facsimile reprints of particular texts are beginning to appear, but usually at prices that place them out of the reach of students. Not till we have separate and substantial selections in affordable paperbacks of the work of individual poets will most readers be able to move beyond the present sense of women's poetry of the period as a rather uneven and jumbled lump to an awareness of it as the work of distinct and differentiated individuals – as is the case with male poets like Blake, Wordsworth and Keats.

Differentiation is the necessary next step because the experience and output of women Romantic poets is wildly varied and cannot be reduced to a single category. I argued in the first chapter that an exciting and distinguishing feature of the literature you are studying is that it comes from and explores the feelings of every level of society, and the same is true when we come to look at women's poetry. In this chapter I will be looking at a poem by Mary Robinson, a woman very much in the public eye when she was mistress of the Prince of Wales and author of a best-selling autobiography, and a poem by Elizabeth Hands, a servant working in Rugby and so deeply obscure that we do not even know the year of her birth or her death.

A more revealing instance of different origins and the difference of outlook that flows from them is contained in the story of the angry, tangled relationship of Hannah More and Ann Yearsley. More, whose huge sales meant that she was able to leave what was then a massive fortune of £30,000 when she died, met Yearsley when the latter came to collect scraps from More's house for use as pig swill. More arranged and supervised the publication of Yearsley's *Poems on Several Occasions* in 1785 and decided that, because Yearsley was a poor dairymaid, the most prudent thing to do was to invest the earnings from sales in a trust fund. Yearsley would be paid the £18 a year interest that derived from the fund. Understandably, Yearsley, happy at first to have found a patron, was furious at being patronised and successfully demanded the right to full access to the money earned by her work. Her fight to control her own income and More's sense that she was best qualified to supervise the life of a milkmaid shows neatly enough that divisions of class are much more important than a coincidence of sex when we come to think about women poets of the period. A sense of that difference will need to be at the centre of any work on them.

This work will not be dictated by a sense that women's poetry ought to be nodded towards, which is every bit as patronising as More's view of Yearsley. Rather, it is determined by an unavoidable statistical fact:

there were 1,402 first editions of volumes of poetry published by women between 1770 and 1835, as J. R. de J. Jackson notes in his *Romantic Poetry by Women: A Bibliography* (1993). This means, quite simply, that most Romantic poets were women. It is hard to see any other reason than sexism for the fact that all of this work has until very recently been quite forgotten and most people's general notion of Romantic poetry is of the so-called Big Six (Blake, Wordsworth, Coleridge, Byron, Shelley and Keats). It certainly cannot be argued that all 1,402 books have been carefully, critically scrutinised and regretfully set aside as inferior, because that has not happened. What seems to have operated instead is a sense, usually unexpressed and untheorised but nonetheless tremendously powerful, that Romantic poetry is something men wrote and women did not because they could not or should not. In turn, that makes the present an enormously exciting time to be studying this period as we watch generations of crass cultural amnesia being replaced by a delighted rediscovery of the full extent of the achievements of the past.

I suggested in the last paragraph that hostility to the notion of women poets was usually unexpressed, but nonetheless there are plenty of examples of overt hostility. In 'The Unsex'd Females: A Poem' published in 1798, the Anglican clergyman Richard Polwhele attacked poets such as Ann Yearsley ('a wanderer from her meads and milk'), Mary Robinson, Anna Barbauld, Helen Maria Williams and Charlotte Smith. He called them 'A female band despising NATURE'S law'. They offered the model of an 'unsex'd woman/ . . . /To Gallic freaks or Gallic faith resigned'. The repeated 'Gallic', in a year when there were genuine fears of a French invasion, is a measure both of Polwhele's unbalanced hysteria and an indication of his sense of their treachery not just to their sex but also to their nation.

Polwhele's hysteria was given calm, official backing. The *Anti-Jacobin Review*, a journal which was secretly subsidised from Government funds, warmly welcomed his poem, commenting in May 1799:

> We find it, at once, politically useful, and poetically beautiful. . . . We are happy to see one of the first poets of the day, one who ranks amongst the foremost for richness of language, vividness of fancy, and brilliance of imagery, employing his poetical talents, at this awful crisis of church and state, in vindication of all that is dear to us as Britons and as Christians.

These words are worth pausing on because they illustrate neatly enough the complex barriers, not just literary but here national and religious too, that stood between women and the writing of poetry.

These were barriers that did not diminish with the years. The Poet Laureate Robert Southey is perhaps these days best remembered for his letter to the young Charlotte Brontë who wrote to him in 1837 for advice as she set out on her career as a writer. He replied:

> Literature cannot be the business of a woman's life, and it ought not to be. The more she is engaged in her proper duties, the less leisure will she have for it, even as an accomplishment and a recreation.

Of course, not everybody agreed with Polwhele and Southey. If that had been the case, 1,402 volumes of women's poetry would not have been published in those years. For every threatened clergyman and pompous Poet Laureate there were by contrast people like Joseph Johnson, the foremost radical publisher of the 1790s, who provided Mary Woll-stonecraft with funds and encouragement to launch her career as a writer. But government support for Polwhele in the shape of friendly reviews and for Southey in his official post as Laureate show the pow-erful strand of prejudice in the dominant culture that women writers in the period had to negotiate their way round if they were to function as writers at all.

It was not just prejudice that made life difficult for women writers. There were also practical problems. Those 'proper duties' of a woman's life that Southey severely recommended to Charlotte Brontë made time and space for writing hard to find, and several women neatly turned that problem into their subject. Anne Grant, an Army chaplain's wife who had twelve children, faced her situation in a poem written in 1795, 'A Familiar Epistle to a Friend':

> Yet our souls are so crusted with housewifely moss
> That Fancy's bright furnace yields nothing but dross:
> Surrounded with balling, and squalling, and prattle,
> With handmaids unhandy, and gossiping tattle,
> Cut fingers to bandage, and stockings to darn,
> And labyrinths endless of ill-managed yarn . . .

The manic accumulation of petty demands conveyed through the five-fold repetition of 'And' offers a glimpse of the sort of frustrations that must have caused many women to give up poetry and carry on tiredly darning fingers and bandaging stockings.

Anne Grant's poem was published by subscription in 1808 in a volume called *The Highlanders and Other Poems*. Subscription publication was extremely common at the time and was the way that most of the women's poems discussed in this chapter first appeared. It is worth thinking about for a moment because although it provided them with an opportunity it also presented them with very real constraints. What happens with subscription publication is that the author (or more often the author's influential friend – Hannah More in the case of Ann Yearsley) gets together a list of people who undertake to buy the volume in question once it is published. This list together with the money pledged can then be taken to a potential publisher. Publishers, who might understandably be reluctant to market work by unknown authors that could incur heavy losses, cannot lose in the case of subscriptions. They are usually quite happy to bring out books with guaranteed sales.

Where the constraint comes in for the writer is the need to produce work that will attract plenty of subscribers. People at that time with sufficient education to read poetry and sufficient spare income to buy it would very largely have been middle-class or upper-class men. To get their signature on a subscription list meant producing material that they would like to read and would not find offensive. Mary Wollstonecraft was able to write and publish *A Vindication of the Rights of Woman* in 1792 because she had met a radical publisher Joseph Johnson who supported the project and was prepared to take a risk with it. It is very unlikely to have been published if she had had to hunt around to find several thousand wealthy gentlemen prepared to back a project which most of them would have seen as a threat to their power and privilege.

When Percy Bysshe Shelley started writing poetry he wrote what he wanted to write and, as the son of an aristocrat with easy access to money or at least to money-lenders, was not constrained by any sense of what the powerful might find acceptable. Thus, in a ballad called 'The Devil's Walk', written when he was nineteen and published at his own expense, he calls the mad King George III 'brainless', notes the 'maudlin brain' of the Prince Regent and accuses the Foreign Secretary Castlereagh of murder. By contrast, a working-class woman like Elizabeth Hands (whose poetry we will be looking at more closely later in the chapter) was only published because a teacher at a public school, Rugby, was prepared to circulate her work amongst his friends and so put together a subscription list. It is doubtful if the schoolmaster and his friends would have been prepared to make the same effort for poems like Shelley's 'The Devil's Walk'. In short, anyone with subscription publication in mind had to reconcile very contradictory demands – on the one hand being true to her experience and inspiration, and on the other hand producing material that was pleasantly acceptable to the gentlemen whose signatures she needed if her work was to appear at all.

It was a demand that understandably defeated a lot of women. If you flip through any of the anthologies of their work now available you will find a lot of poetry that is timid, uninspired, conventional and unthreatening. It is the sort of verse that you can see a charitably minded vicar or a teacher in a kindly moment being prepared to put his name to as one of the subscribers, a list of whose names was generally printed at the front of the volume when it was eventually published. If some of the poetry now becoming available for study seems to students flat and disappointing – and that is certainly my experience of a lot of student response – then we need to remember that this tells us more about the nature of the poetry market than it does about the abilities and talents of the women forced to work within its boundaries.

One way of working within those boundaries was to make patient attempts to extend them. Again and again we see women writers drawing attention to and making poetry out of the apparent trivialities of domestic experience to which many of them were confined and with which most men were unfamiliar. Poems such as Anna Barbauld's 'Washing Day' (1797), Elizabeth Moody's 'To a Lady, Who Sent the Author a Present of a Fashionable Bonnet' (1798) or Helen Maria Williams's 'To Mrs K–, On Her Sending Me an English Christmas Plum-Cake at Paris' (1823) observe the bits and pieces of women's day-to-day social life with wry humour. They seem to me to be another part of that democratic drive in Romantic literature to widen the awareness and sympathies of readers that we have noted in earlier chapters.

Some are more ambitious. Anna Barbauld's 'To a Little Invisible Being Who Is Expected Soon to Become Visible' (1795) has a title that is irritatingly coy to twenty-first century readers, but push past that and you find a powerful exploration of the contradictory emotions and ambiguous desires of a pregnant woman. Similarly mixed and strong feelings are displayed in Anne Hunter's 'To My Daughter On Being Separated from Her on Her Marriage' (1802). Dorothy Wordsworth's 'The Mother's Return' (1807) follows the attempts of a woman baby-sitting two young children to try to cope with their incoherent excitement on the eve of their mother's return. All three poems are about profound and central human sentiments, yet sentiments very rarely described or analysed in the overwhelmingly masculine discourse of previous literature.

To join a discourse and at the same time to break it up and to change it is not an easy thing to do. Just occasionally we find a woman writing a poem that is open and explicit about that task. Anna Barbauld's 'To Mr. [S.T.] C[oleridge]' is one of the most acute and tactful critiques of

Coleridge's work ever published, yet it appeared in 1799, very early in Coleridge's career and only a few months after the publication of *Lyrical Ballads*. The poem imagines a 'hill of science' with 'steep/And rugged paths'. Halfway up it there is a 'grove' into which the tired climber might be tempted. It is a grove full of 'tangled mazes', 'strange enchantment' and 'dubious shapes' in 'dim glades'. Nothing is substantial: it is all 'Dreams . . . mystic visions . . . mists . . . huge shadows . . . floating gossamer . . . dreamy twilight . . . moonbeam rainbows'. It is a place where 'Indolence . . . wears the garb/Of deep philosophy.' Turning at last to Coleridge, she addresses him directly:

> Youth beloved
> Of Science – of the Muse beloved, – not here,
> Not in the maze of metaphysic lore,
> Build thou thy resting place!

In 1799 it seems to me that Anna Barbauld is astonishingly perceptive about precisely those places where Coleridge was to spend much of the next thirty-five years. More than that, she describes a space where she sees one of the most exciting young male poets of the 1790s heading and marks it out as 'dangerous ground'.

The poem ends disappointingly, with brief and schoolmasterly advice about the ground that poets should choose instead (namely 'fair exertion . . . /For friends, for country'). I'd like to spend the rest of this chapter looking more precisely at the ground women poets, in particular Elizabeth Hands and Mary Robinson, chose to occupy. I have picked them out from their contemporaries simply because I have found that students enjoy their work the most.

II

As I have already mentioned, we know so little about Elizabeth Hands that we are not even sure when she was born or when she died. Most of the available facts about her are gathered together in a single-page biographical note in Roger Lonsdale's anthology of eighteenth-century women poets. There we find that she was a servant working for a family in Allesly, a village a few miles west of Coventry, and it was in the *Coventry Mercury* that she published poems under the pen name of Daphne. She then married a blacksmith with a forge in Bourton near Rugby. Philip Bracebridge Homer, an assistant master at Rugby School, was the moving spirit behind the successful subscription list that financed the publication of her only book, *The Death of Amnon. A Poem. With An Appendix; Containing Pastorals, and Other Poetical Pieces*, which appeared in 1789. In the Preface she says accurately enough that she was 'born in obscurity . . . never emerging beyond the lower stations in life'. That is underlined by the fact that, apart from a couple of reviews of the volume in the *Gentleman's Magazine* (June 1790) and the *Monthly Review* (November 1790), she then disappeared from literary history as quietly as she entered it.

The volume itself has never been reprinted, but we can now begin to look again at some of the poems of this remarkable working-class woman thanks to the selections printed in both Roger Lonsdale's and Jennifer Breen's anthologies. A few are the sort of standard subscription volume verse noted earlier in this chapter: inoffensive lines likely to secure the support of the unoffended wealthy. For example, the titles of 'The Favourite Swain' and 'Lob's Courtship' tell us most of what we need to know about the poems. There is conventional eighteenth-century poetic diction in the title of the former: 'swain' is an archaic term for a young male lover and particularly useful for uninspired versifiers because it rhymes with the sort of experiences – (pain, gain), weather encountered by (rain) and places inhabited by (plain) – had by such a lover. Hands uses most of those rhymes as well as many other tired poeticisms ('generous muse . . . woodbine bower . . . artless youth . . . flowery lawn . . . lowly rill'). 'Lob's Courtship' is no better and again the title gives it away: 'Lob' was an all-purpose name for a country bumpkin or clown, much like 'Wally' was a few years ago, and the poem is every bit as patronising as its title. It tells us little about Hands's abilities and a lot about the normal prejudices of eighteenth-century bards and their subscribers.

But much more interesting than this timid stuff is a pair of sharply funny pieces called 'A Poem, on the Supposition of an Advertisement Appearing in a Morning Paper, of the Publication of a Volume of Poems, by a Servant-Maid' and 'A Poem, on the Supposition of the Book Having Been Published and Read'. If 'Lob's Courtship' was weak because it merely echoed upper-class condescension, these two poems are brilliant because of the way they satirise it. As a servant-maid herself, Hands anticipates what her social superiors might make of her daring to publish poetry. Some of those self-appointed superiors are dimly philistine, others plain ignorant and no one responds with the taste, decency or sensitivity that they lay claim to. A few are just nasty:

'For my part I think,' says old Lady Marr-Joy,
'A servant might find herself other employ:
Was she mine I'd employ her as long as 'twas light,
And send her to bed without candle at night.'

The words are brave for the way that they directly confront rather than
slip unobtrusively past the bigotry of many of her potential readers. She
refuses to accept unthinkingly the cramped circumstances which determine the distribution and reception of her poems. Instead, she stands
aside from those circumstances and, viewing them critically, turns them
into the very subject of those poems. Readers come expecting to look
at a view and are disconcerted to find that they face a mirror, and a
deliberately unflattering one at that.

III

I noted earlier the way that many women poets of the period tried
to expand their readers' awareness by forcing them to look at the
trivialities of domestic life. There are good examples of that in Elizabeth Hands's volume, for example some comic verses entitled 'Written,
originally extempore, on seeing a Mad Heifer run through the Village
where the Author lives'. And the poem I want to look at in detail faces
domesticity without sentimentality. It is called 'On an Unsociable
Family':

O what a strange parcel of creatures are we,
Scarce ever to quarrel, or even agree;
We all are alone, though at home altogether,
Except to the fire constrained by the weather;
Then one says, ''Tis cold', which we all of us know,
And with unanimity answer, ''Tis so':
With shrugs and with shivers all look at the fire,
And shuffle ourselves and our chairs a bit nigher;
Then quickly, preceded by silence profound,
A yawn epidemical catches around:
Like social companions we never fall out,
Nor ever care what one another's about
To comfort each other is never our plan,
For to please ourselves, truly, is more than we can.

I   Look for the main idea or feeling

As we have seen several times already, Hands's titles are often and unsurprisingly a straightforward description of the subject matter of the following poem, and this one is no exception. It says it is about an unsociable family, and that is the idea the poem presents. The fourteen lines look in a variety of ways at the different sorts of tension and contradiction that exist inside such a family.

So much is so obvious that in one sense it might seem scarcely worth noting. And yet, if you think about it, it is remarkable. That is not the way the family is normally presented in the best-known literature of the period. More characteristically it is constructed as a place of refuge from rather than the site of such tensions and contradictions. This is not the place to give a full and nuanced history of the representation of the family in late eighteenth- and early nineteenth-century literature, but if we think for a moment of the work of two of the most famous women writers of that time then the picture is certainly very different. All six of Jane Austen's novels, which began to appear in the decade after Hands's volume, are arguably about the successful attempt of the heroine to found a perfect family. The plots of those novels are usually made up of several wrong turns taken by the heroine and they are often filled with disastrously dysfunctional families from the Dashwoods in her first published novel *Sense and Sensibility* to the Elliots in her last, *Persuasion*. But with the marriage of heroine to hero in the final pages the suggestion is clear that the experience of the previous chapters has given them the wisdom to found an ideal family that will be the basis of their subsequent happiness.

There is a parallel presentation of the family as the key both to individual fulfilment and social cohesion in Mary Shelley's *Frankenstein*, published in 1818. *Frankenstein*, of course, is about many things, as the twentieth-century film industry discovered to its immense profit. But the original Preface, written by Mary's husband Percy, describes the novel as, amongst other things, an 'exhibition of the amiableness of domestic affection', and you can see what he was driving at if you look at what happens in the book. Running through the text is a clear sense that when Frankenstein isolates himself and cuts himself off from family ties to pursue his private scientific ambitions, then literally and metaphorically he creates a monster. He then refuses to create a stabilising family for the monster by destroying the creature's half-made partner, so the monster in his turn smashes Frankenstein's attempt to start a new family of his own by murdering Frankenstein's bride on their wedding night. Without the stability of family life, the text on one level implies that society is in danger of collapsing into a war of mindlessly competitive males with women as their principal victims.

Which is not what 'On an Unsociable Family' wants to say. Hands sets out to offer a very different picture of family life, its frustrations and tedium, and does so with a down-to-earth realism that is a long way from the sentimental portraits provided by many of her Romantic and Victorian successors.

2   Look at the choices and combinations of words that express the main idea or feeling

The frustrations felt by this unsociable family are mainly conveyed in the poem through a series of irritating contradictions. The members of the family rarely quarrel and yet they rarely agree (l. 2). When they are all together, they are yet at the same time 'all . . . alone' (l. 3). They 'never fall out' but at the same time they don't 'care what one another's about' (ll. 11–12). These contradictions are imaged and centred by the contrast of fire and surrounding cold that lies in the middle of the poem.

Various devices are used to underline the tedium of this existence. About the only thing they really share is the 'yawn' that spreads like an epidemic (l. 11). Each line is heavily end-stopped; that is, the reader is slowed at the conclusion of every line by heavy punctuation. (You can see the effect of this if you go back to Chapter 4 and contrast it with the passage from *The Prelude* where we saw Wordsworth conveying the sheer speed and exhilaration of skating through a series of run-on lines which meant that the reader, like the skater, rarely paused.) Here the movement is deliberately slow, monotonous and repetitive.

The sense of repetition is further emphasised by the fact that the fourteen lines are in fact seven pairs of rhymed couplets. You can see the effect of that if you try reading the poem aloud: the evenly spaced pauses forced by the end-stopping serve to underline the rhymes, so that you hear the seven echoes with plonking clarity and predictability.

The fact that this effect is very deliberate is brought home when we realise that Hands is writing a sonnet, and yet to achieve this effect she breaks many of the rules of sonnet-writing. The sonnet is perhaps the most famous of all lyric forms. It is fourteen lines long and in English it normally took one of two forms. First was the Petrarchan sonnet, which is divided into an eight-line followed by a six-line section with a rhyme-scheme of *abba abba cde cde*. Alternatively there is the form preferred by Shakespeare, with three quatrains (four-line stanzas) and a concluding couplet. This formal arrangement normally structures the content of the poem, so that in a Petrarchan sonnet you describe a problem in the first eight lines and you try to meet it in some way in the final six. In the Shakespearean sonnet the three stanzas tend to describe a situation in a variety of ways and then the final two lines seek some sort of epigrammatic answer or conclusion. Both forms of sonnet were developed by major English male poets like Shakespeare, Spenser, Sidney, Milton and Wordsworth into a major lyric vehicle for the exploration of the self and its relation to the rest of the world.

One of the most remarkable features of the literature of the Romantic period is the way women like Anna Seward and Charlotte Smith take up this form largely developed by men and use it to explore female desire and female experience. What is interesting in the example by Elizabeth Hands we are looking at is that, although she sticks with the fourteen-line form of the sonnet, she experiments technically by ditching the internal arrangements of both Petrarch and Shakespeare. Instead, she opts for seven couplets, something that might seem trivial to us but which would have struck a poetry reader in 1789 as extremely odd. The effect is to bar the sort of progress which we have seen as being built into the Petrarchan and Shakespearean sonnet. Rather than their pattern of problem/resolution, difficulty/response the pattern we have here is of monotonous repetition. We go round and round the problem and are no nearer a solution in line 14 than we were in line 1. The family remain locked in their unfulfilling circle.

3 Focus on the lines which clinch your sense of the poem's main idea or feeling

The end of a sonnet is the place where readers normally look for its final message, so it is worth closer examination:

> To comfort each other is never our plan,
> For to please ourselves, truly, is more than we can.

The bracketing commas make us hesitate for a second as we read 'truly' in the last line, and that alerts us to the fact that the whole line can be read in two ways. It could mean 'To please ourselves truly (that is, fully/adequately) is more than we are able to do', or it could mean 'Truly (that is, it is true to say that) we are not able to please ourselves'. The one meaning reinforces the other to give a sense of deeply dissatisfied people.

What we have in the two lines are two statements – 'to comfort each other' and 'to please ourselves' – that are linked together by the conjunction 'For', whose use in this sense implies that what follows is the cause of what precedes. Thus one inability ('to comfort each other') is seen as a function of another ('to please ourselves'). These people are not able to function as a community and provide each other with comfort and the reason they cannot do that is that they are not fulfilled as separate individuals. The two incapacities are mutually reinforcing and that is the real horror of life in this family. Its members experience neither the benefits of sociability nor the consolations of personal autonomy because the family stands in the way of both. That perhaps is the reason why Hands chooses to break from the strict form of Petrarchan or Shakespearean sonnets with their suggestion of movement and progress. What she offers instead is a portrait of a family circled round a fire who in another sense are locked in a circle of relationships that diminish them and from which there seems no escape.

4   Sum up your impressions of the poem as a whole

What we have in this sonnet is a picture of a family unsociable, bored and dissatisfied. So much is clear from what the poem says. It is also, as I argued earlier in this book, sometimes worth thinking about what a poem does *not* say. Looking at this one again, I am struck by the fact that we end the poem with no idea how many people there are in this family, what their names are, their ages, their sex. And yet, if asked to describe yourself to a stranger, your name, age and sex are probably the things you would start with because they are central to most people's sense of themselves and their identity. The people here have no distinct identities. They are presented as a family lump without separate individualities and indeed they are scarcely human: rather 'a strange parcel of creatures', as the first line calls them. That is central to their problems of apathy and alienation.

Fourteen lines do not offer enough room for anyone to develop a philosophy of life and, as we have seen earlier, the lyric is not the place to do that anyway, so it would be presumptuous to suggest that this sonnet represents Hands's view of family life. She does generalise the portrait to some extent by using the indefinite ('an') rather than the definite article ('the') in the title. And there are other poems in this volume that show women resisting the offer to start a family. In 'Perplexity: A Poem', for example, the female speaker is torn between two lovers, Collin and Damon, and refuses to make a choice, while in 'The Widower's Courtship' Nell cheerfully turns down the widower's proposal. There is perhaps just enough evidence there to link Elizabeth Hands with other brave thinkers in the following decade like Blake, Godwin and Wollstonecraft who began to think critically about the family and speculate about other forms of relationship.

IV

Nowadays Mary Robinson is as obscure as Elizabeth Hands, but in her time and on several occasions since she has been famous. Coleridge, the leading literary critic of the day, told Southey in 1800 that 'she is a woman of undoubted genius' and her contemporary sales and popularity suggest that many people shared that view. Unlike Hands who, as we have seen, vanished almost before she had properly appeared, Robinson's memory ought to have been secured by her posthumous *Memoirs*, edited and published by her daughter Mary Elizabeth in 1801. And subsequently there have been at least two biographies: M. Steen's *The Lost One: A Biography of Mary Robinson* which came out in 1937 and, in 1957, R. D. Bass's *The Green Dragoon: The Lives of Banastre Tarleton and Mary Robinson*. But the kind of cultural amnesia that we have seen befalling women Romantic poets enveloped her too, and until she began appearing again in anthologies in the 1990s a whole generation was quite ignorant of her and her work.

A strange fact, granted that both the quality of her work and the nature of her life fascinate those modern readers who come across them. She was born in Bristol on 27 November 1758 in a cottage which she describes in her memoirs as 'supported by the mouldering arches of the cloister, dark, Gothic' that belonged to a ruined monastery. It was an oddly apt start because her tempestuous life that followed was supported but more often undermined by her contact with a series of mouldering arches in the shape of four ruinous men. First, her father, Captain John Darby, a sailor whose constant absences pushed the family into financial problems that made them ready to accept a marriage proposal when Mary was only fifteen from Thomas Robinson, an articled clerk at Lincoln's Inn. They were probably helped in their decision by the fact that Mary was eight weeks pregnant on her wedding day. Thomas

Robinson turned out to be another mouldering ruin rather than a support and the following year was arrested for debts of £1,200 which meant that Mary and her new baby Mary Elizabeth spent the next ten months with him in the King's Bench Prison. The spell in prison at least gave her time to write and to plan her next career move. On her release she was engaged as an actress at Drury Lane Theatre where in 1799 the Prince of Wales saw her in a production of *The Winter's Tale* and she became his mistress. Being mistress to a fool is as precarious as being wife to a wastrel and, following enormous press interest in the affair, she soon found herself abandoned again. It was a few years later in 1782 that she committed herself to the most spectacular ruin of all, Colonel Banastre Tarleton. Tarleton was a compulsive gambler with desperate debts who eventually deserted her in 1798 when he spotted a rich young heiress to marry. Before that, in 1783, he had left Mary when she was pregnant and in the course of her journey after him she miscarried. A result of the miscarriage was partial paralysis of the legs (which she dismissed as 'trifling lameness') for the rest of her life. She died aged forty-two in 1800 leaving her daughter to publish her uncompleted *Memoirs* in 1801. Her death at the turn of the century was in a way as oddly apt as her birth: most nineteenth-century readers regarded her life as an eighteenth-century disgrace and it was not till the twentieth century that people began to look again with interest at her and her work.

What strikes us now is the way that, despite all the wreckage of her life, she wrote, even from her teenage years. She wrote of necessity, to support her daughter, to ease herself out of the piles of her debts and her husband's. She wrote therefore what she hoped would sell, and initially that meant largely rubbish: derivative rubbish, imitative rubbish, the kind of stuff that readers seemed to be buying or that subscribers would sign up to. Any kind of stuff: poems, novels, plays, essays, memoirs. And the wonder is that through it all and out of it all she slowly found her own voice. In the last decade of her life wrote with an angry clarity and honest insight that makes her subsequent neglect much more of a scandal than the sad details of her life.

What that life taught her was politics. It is increasingly out of that politics that she wrote. Contact with the Prince of Wales on the one hand and the King's Bench Prison on the other taught her about class and about the disparities of power and wealth in her society, and all of that goes into the making of a poem like 'The Birth-Day' (1800). Here she generates immense power out of the enraged juxtaposition of 'The pampered Countess' with 'the wretched poor', 'Great names, adorning little souls' with 'Pale Misery', 'The senseless Duchess' with 'the beggar freezing', 'high-born-fools' with 'the pining infant'.

Increasingly at the core of this politics is a principled feminism, a brave place to take a stand at a time when it was commercial death to do so. Her *A Letter to the Women of England, on the Injustice of Mental Subordination* (1799) goes out of its way to pay tribute to her friend Mary Wollstonecraft as 'an illustrious British female (whose death has not been sufficiently lamented, but to whose genius posterity will render justice)'. The truculent defensiveness of that compliment points to her awareness of the fact that by 1799 Wollstonecraft's name was scarcely mentionable in polite society. She reproduces some of Wollstonecraft's arguments from *A Vindication of the Rights of Woman* (1792) because 'it requires a *legion of Wollstonecrafts* to undermine the poisons of prejudice and malevolence'. But she moves beyond them too, deploring 'the drudgery of domestic life' and calling for the establishment of a 'UNIVERSITY FOR WOMEN'.

Her feminism comes through too in her major poetic work of the 1790s, her sequence of forty-four sonnets entitled *Sappho and Phaon*. She frames the work with a Preface that makes her project clear: it is to pay tribute 'to the talents of my illustrious countrywomen who, unpatronised by Courts, and unprotected by the powerful, persevere in the paths of literature'. A following note 'To the Reader' explains her choice of subject matter and her approach to it:

> Ovid and Pope have celebrated the passion of Sappho for Phaon, but their portraits, however beautifully finished, are replete with shades tending rather to depreciate than to adorn the Grecian poetess [. . . .] I have endeavoured to collect, in the succeeding pages, the most liberal accounts of that illustrious woman whose fame has transmitted to us some fragments of her works through many dark ages, and for the space of more than 2,000 years.

In the twentieth century Sappho, born in Lesbos and flourishing around the middle of the seventh century BC, became a lesbian icon. Robinson's aim is different: the above quotations and the 'Account of Sappho' with which she prefaces the sequence make it clear that she is offering Sappho as a model for women writers in hard times.

Robinson's experience of poverty and exploitation meant that she was a natural supporter of the campaign for the abolition of slavery. The cause succeeded seven years after Robinson's death when the House of Commons, after several previous failures, finally passed a bill abolishing the slave trade. It was a cause that inspired some remarkable work. For example, Blake included 'The Little Black Boy' in *Songs of Innocence and of Experience* (1794), a moving account of the way the world seemed through the eyes of a black boy. In 'The Negro Girl' (1800) Robinson creates out of her feminism a view of the world through the eyes of a black female slave. In the poem Zelma watches while her lover Draco is drowned with fellow slaves in a stormy shipwreck. The two basic situations – slavery and a shipwreck – combine to produce an extraordinary sense of Zelma's impotence, a woman standing alone against the overwhelming power of both 'the angry waves' and 'the tyrant white man'. Yet in the face of all that the poem is given over to Zelma's magnificently defiant shout of protest.

V

The poem by Mary Robinson that I'd like to look at in more detail is called 'January, 1795'.

> Pavement slippery, people sneezing,
> Lords in ermine, beggars freezing;
> Titled gluttons dainties carving,
> Genius in a garret starving.
>
> Lofty mansions, warm and spacious;   5
> Courtiers cringing and voracious;
> Misers scarce the wretched heeding;
> Gallant soldiers fighting, bleeding.
>
> Wives who laugh at passive spouses;
> Theatres, and meeting houses;   10
> Balls, where simpering misses languish;
> Hospitals, and groans of anguish.
>
> Arts and sciences bewailing;
> Commerce drooping, credit failing;
> Placemen mocking subjects loyal;   15
> Separations, weddings royal.
>
> Authors who can't earn a dinner;
> Many a subtle rogue a winner;

Fugitives for shelter seeking;
Misers hoarding, tradesmen breaking.   20

Taste and talents quite deserted;
All the laws of truth perverted;
Arrogance o'er merit soaring;
Merit silently deploring.

Ladies gambling night and morning;   25
Fools the work of genius scorning;
Ancient dames for girls mistaken,
Youthful damsels quite forsaken.

Some in luxury delighting;
More in talking than in fighting;   30
Lovers old, and beaux decrepid;
Lordlings empty and insipid.

Poets, painters, and musicians;
Lawyers, doctors, politicians:
Pamphlets, newspapers, and odes,   35
Seeking fame by different roads.

Gallant souls with empty purses,
Generals only fit for nurses;
School-boys, smit with martial spirit,
Taking place of veteran merit.   40

Honest men who can't get places,
Knaves who show unblushing faces;
Ruin hastened, peace retarded;
Candour spurned, and art rewarded.

I   Look for the main idea or feeling

This poem was first published in a London daily newspaper, the *Morning Post*, on 29 January 1795, so the poem's title 'January, 1795' and its context in a daily paper is designed to give its first readers the impression that here is a view of their city today. The first word or two in most stanzas catches sight of different people ('Wives . . .', 'Authors . . .',

'Honest men . . .') and different places ('Pavement . . .', 'Lofty mansions . . .') and suggests a quick sketch of that city, its scenes and its citizens caught on the very day the paper was printed.

The war between Britain and France had started in February 1793 and hence as we might expect Robinson notes the extent to which the capital city after two years of armed conflict has been militarised: 'soldiers' in the second stanza, 'Generals' and 'School-boys, smit with martial spirit' in the tenth. But more than those direct references I think we get a sense that her main conception of the impact of war on London is one of gross incongruities. Right from the beggars alongside the lords in the poem's second line, we see that the poem's main idea is that London has become a city of intolerable contradictions generated by the conflict with France and the economic strains that it causes. Every stanza works with some sort of massive disparity, from the powerful and the wretched in these first lines to the 'Honest men' and 'Knaves' in the last.

2 Look at the choices and combinations of words that express the main idea or feeling

If we take the first two lines of the poem and re-write them as a piece of normal prose narrative, we come up with something like this: 'The pavement is slippery and the people are sneezing; Lords are in ermine while the beggars are freezing'. What Robinson has done here to turn prose into poetry is to cut out all unnecessary words: definite articles ('the'), auxiliary verbs ('Is', 'are') and conjunctions ('and', 'while'). The result is a dense, sinewy mass of nouns, adjectives and participles, and this is a technique she uses more or less all the way through the poem. So, for example, the last two lines of the second stanza are a condensed version of 'The misers are scarcely heeding the wretched whilst the gallant soldiers are fighting and bleeding.' This kind of pared-down language producing a muscular poetry with all weak or inessential words removed is something that Gerard Manley Hopkins is normally credited with pioneering a couple of generations later and something that many twentieth-century poets have followed. Yet here is Robinson doing precisely that in 1795, and it is something that she experiments with in several later poems written in the last two years of her life such as 'Modern Female Fashions', 'Modern Male Fashions' and 'Winkfield Plain'. For me the effect here is to create a very powerful sense of a cramped, crowded place. Both the city and the language used to describe it have all the normal spaces and leisurely connections removed so that the words, like the people and the buildings, are jammed tight up against each other.

Another remarkable feature of the poem's language is the frequency of present participles. There are four ('sneezing . . . freezing . . . carving . . . starving') that provide a quadruple rhyme in the very first stanza, and two more provide a pair of rhymes in six of the next seven stanzas. There is simply too much of this to be accidental and it is plainly deliberate. What it suggests to me is someone standing at a street corner quickly jotting down notes of what he or she sees – 'dog running, bus passing, people chatting, ostrich exploding' – the sort of thing you might then take home and expand into a considered account. But Robinson is writing for a newspaper and what I think she is trying to keep is that urban sense of immediacy that gets lost once you sit down at a desk and turn your sketchy notes into a carefully worked poem. The result, I think, is an amazing text, an impressionistic montage of the modern city that is normally thought of as one of the original achievements of artists and writers working a hundred years and more after Robinson's death.

3   Focus on the lines which clinch your sense of the poem's main idea or feeling

The last lines are our final memory of a short text so it is often here that poets take care to convey their ideas or feelings most succinctly. Robinson closes by saying:

> Honest men who can't get places,
> Knaves who show unblushing faces;
> Ruin hastened, peace retarded;
> Candour spurned, and art rewarded.

Perhaps the first thing to get out of the way here is that in this instance Robinson uses 'art' in a negative sense to mean artfulness or cunning and not in the more common sense which she uses in the fourth stanza ('Arts and sciences bewailing') where it means various sorts of aesthetic skill such as writing, painting, sculpture and so on. What each of these four lines repetitively suggests is a world turned upside down. In a healthy society we would expect honest men to be employed and knaves to be embarrassed, but here it is the opposite. In normal circumstances we would expect the end of the war to be hastened and ruin to be retarded, but in January 1795 things work the other way round and so in the last line it is the cunning rather than the candid who are rewarded. If, as we have seen already, Robinson makes one of the first attempts to get to grips with life in a city by technically adjusting her poetry, here she gives us one of the first analyses of urban estrangement, the sense that ordinary people are not at ease because everything seems to operate the wrong way round.

And yet this is not the way it always has to be. Robinson does not offer what nowadays have become tired clichés about the eternal inevitability of metropolitan alienation. Instead, her title reminds us that she is talking very specifically about January 1795. Six months earlier she had seen the capital very differently in a poem called 'London's Summer Morning'. Here is how it starts:

Who has not waked to list the busy sounds
Of summer's morning in the sultry smoke
Of noisy London? On the pavement hot
The sooty chimney-boy, with dingy face
And tattered covering, shrilly bawls his trade,
Rousing the sleeping housemaid. At the door
The milk-pail rattles, and the tinkling bell
Proclaims the dustman's office; while the street
Is lost in clouds impervious. Now begins

. . . and so on. The point I want to make here is that this opening gives a wonderful sense of the city waking and beginning to move. One of the ways Robinson achieves this effect is with the use of run-on lines; only one of the nine here has any punctuation at the end, so that the reader moves rapidly through the passage.

'January, 1795' is quite different. Every line in this last stanza we are looking at has heavy punctuation at the end, and so indeed does every line in the poem. Again what we are seeing is a feature that is so frequent that it is plainly deliberate. The speed and movement of London that Robinson captured in the summer of 1794 has gone. After another six months of war and deep into winter, the mood has changed. The end-stopping means there is no momentum, and the earlier poem's sense of people going busily about their work is replaced in these last lines by a perversely stagnant world in which honesty is unemployed and peace retarded. The only thing that is hastening any more is 'Ruin'.

4   Sum up your impressions of the poem as a whole

So what we have in front of us is a poem written for a London newspaper which experiments technically and compacts its words tightly.
The result is a sketch of a city where the speaker's feelings are tensed
by the jarring disparities and reversals that crowd her poem.

   In *Romantics, Rebels and Reactionaries*, Marilyn Butler has noted the
gloom that settled on radical writers in the mid 1790s. Paine had vanished into exile, poets like Blake and Yearsley fell temporarily silent and,
as Godwin puts it in the October 1795 Preface to his novel *Things as
They Are: The Adventures of Caleb Williams*, 'Terror was the order of the
day, and it was feared that even the humble novelist might be shown
to be constructively a traitor.' The hopes inspired in many by the French
Revolution in 1789 had given way to a war between Britain and France
during which poets like Wordsworth, Coleridge and Southey began
their long march from the revolutionary politics of their youth. In one
sense, Robinson's poem is a part of that gloom. We have moved some
distance from the delighted optimism with which, as we have, seen
Paine had closed *Rights of Man* in 1791, exclaiming 'Spring has
begun'; it is deep winter in more senses than the literal one in 'January,
1795'.

   There was a market in the late eighteenth century for melancholic
texts by sensitive women, a market well supplied by poets like Anna
Seward and Charlotte Smith. Mary Robinson wrote for that market too,
but I do not find that poems like 'Stanzas Written after Successive
Nights of Melancholy Dreams' (1793) or 'The Progress of Melancholy'
(1796) work for most modern readers. Perhaps that is because of an
impression that once a writer is able to step outside her depression and
become thoughtfully articulate and metrically precise about it then that
depression comes across as neither deep nor genuine. 'January, 1795'
seems to me to be better than that because there is more to it than
private gloom. She searches out the social roots of what she experiences
as personal depression. The result is a generously angry poem, a poem
of protest on behalf of honest men and beggars and fugitives, right-
eously disgusted at the antics of 'titled gluttons' and 'courtiers cring-
ing'. Robinson's voice has not been muted by the reverses of the early
1790s. Just as, at the end of that decade, she bravely published *A Letter
to the Women of England, on the Injustice of Mental Subordination* at a time
when most readers were no longer interested in feminist arguments, so
here too in 'January, 1795' she writes an enraged indictment of the

capital city when in January 1795 what many subscribers to the *Morning Post* were moving towards was a mix of piety and patriotism. That is what I think in the end makes it such a great poem. It is not trying to be fashionable or acceptable. It takes vigorous hold of language and changes it in order to bring it closer to the feel of life in the new city, and at the same time it uses that language to say something necessary and neglected on behalf of its most powerless citizens. From inmate of a debtor's prison to intimate of the Prince of Wales, Mary Robinson had experienced most things that London had to offer. She draws on the full range of that experience to generate the tensed contradictions that power this text.

VI

Most women in the late eighteenth and early nineteenth century spent most of their lives in a domestic space. In 'On an Unsociable Family', as we have seen, Elizabeth Hands, like many contemporary female poets, reflects on that space. But in the very act of reflecting she moves outside that space to begin to think about the politics of the family. In 'January, 1795', Mary Robinson thinks beyond that again to the politics of London and the whole nation. In miniature, these two poems seem to me to delineate the work of women writers in this period. They begin in a distinct and different position to which they are assigned by their sex. But in the best of their work they do not remain confined within that position but instead use it as a vantage point to view the rest of the world and to view it from different angles, angles as widely varied as that of a patronised servant or a discarded royal mistress.

As we read and study more and more of this poetry by women it is becoming clear that it will not do to see it as an interesting footnote to previous notions of Romantic literature. Nor is it stimulating background reading with all the relegation into the unfocused distance that the term 'background' implies. Old and narrow generalisations about Romanticism, its concerns and its values will fall away as manifestly untrue and indeed the very term 'Romantic' itself will perhaps have to be discarded, as several recent critics have argued, because it was made out of a series of assumptions that the evidence no longer supports. It is increasingly being replaced by neutral labels like 'late eighteenth- and early nineteenth-century writing' or 'literature from 1780 to 1830', certainly not very snappy terms but much looser ones, able to accommodate the diversity and the contradictions of the culture of the time. As we read our way into those complexities and the challenges to understanding, that they generate we begin to realise that there has never been a more exciting time than the present for studying and revisualising this particular piece of the past.

8

WRITING AN ESSAY

FIRST the bad news. There is no Golden Rule for Writing Successful Essays that this book or any other can provide. It would make life a lot simpler if there were, especially when you are faced with a question on, say, *The Prelude* and are unsure whether to count the metaphors, speculate libellously about Wordsworth's relationship with his sister, or settle for a niftily disguised version of what the editor says in the preface. Which of the many possibilities you choose to pursue depends in the end on why you think the subject is worth bothering with at all. It depends, in other words, on some sort of theory, however rudimentary and unacknowledged, of what literature is and what place its study occupies or ought to occupy in society.

What I have tried to do in this book is to supply you with a method that lets you read Romantic poems in such a way that you can accumulate your own material and then construct your essays out of that material. But even that method is not neutral or theoretically innocent. It is based on the insistence, in Chapter 1, that texts only have meaning in contexts and that a close reading of Romantic poems has to work from a sense of the time when the poems were produced, a view not shared by all literary critics. It is simply not possible to read a text and begin to say anything about it without a theory of some sort, without some sense of what is worth saying, of what needs to be examined and of what can be ignored as irrelevant. And once you choose a theory then it will become obvious that what you are doing to texts is not so much uncovering meanings that are unproblematically there but rather helping to create them as you work with authors to make their words speak.

What I have touched on in the last two paragraphs are some of the critical issues that have fuelled debates around, for example, Marxism, feminism, structuralism and deconstruction, which have in their turn revolutionised and revitalised the practice of literary criticism in recent years. The result of that revolution is that there is no stable consensus as there seemed to be a generation ago about what constitutes the subject of English Literature or about what constitutes literary criticism, whether it takes the form of a book on the life and work of Keats or an essay on 'To Autumn'. The subject, like the society in which it is implicated, is a site on which contending claims for truth and meaning meet and struggle. That is part of the reason why the subject is worth studying, but also part of the reason why Golden Rules for producing critical essays do not exist.

What I have done so far in this book, then, is to work from a theory and present a method for reading Romantic poetry that would generate ideas and things to say. What I shall try to do in the rest of the chapter is to suggest ways of organising those ideas into effective answers to the questions that you will meet.

THE QUESTION

To begin at the beginning. You need to answer the question you have actually been asked rather than one you would rather have been asked. Resist the understandable temptation, almost inevitable under the pressure of examination nerves, to write down everything you can remember about Keats as an easy alternative to confronting the specific demands of the question in front of you. Everything you can remember about Keats will certainly be useful, but not all of it will be relevant to a question on, for example, his major odes. Your knowledge has to be taken hold of, selected, reordered and shaped so that it ends up as a clear response to the issues raised by your essay title. And the best way to do that is to let the question provoke you into *thinking* about Keats rather than using it as a peg on which to hang what you know about him.

How do you do that? Well, one way is to interrogate the question: that is, look at some of the terms the question uses and ask yourself what they mean. Take, for instance, this question on Coleridge:

'However remote the world which we enter in Coleridge's poetry may seem, we never lose touch with our familiar one.' Have you found this to be true?

There are several problems here, not least the assumption that 'we' all share a 'familiar' world. But the key term when it comes to answering the question is surely 'remote'. 'Remote' in what sense? You might think of such poems as the 'Sonnets on Eminent Characters', whose subjects (Burke, Pitt, Koskiusko and so on) are historically remote; or 'Hymn before Sun-rise, in the Vale of Chamouni,' whose setting is geographically remote; or 'The Rime of the Ancient Mariner', which voyages to the remotest edges of the unconscious mind; or 'Kubla Khan', which draws on remote myth and legend; or 'Religious Musings', which deals with aspects of Christian doctrine now remote from most readers' experience; or 'Fire, Famine, and Slaughter', an adaptation of Virgilian eclogues and so drawing on a remote classical tradition. You may choose to explore a variety of ways in which the world of Coleridge's poetry is remote, or you may decide to fix on just one of them. But you need to indicate from the outset that 'remote' can be read legitimately in several ways and how *you* are going to interpret it, if your essay is to avoid floundering indecisively between the various possible interpretations of the term. So the best start to an answer is often to begin by asking questions of the question itself rather than by plunging straight ahead and realising by about page three that, because some of the question's assumptions are problematic, you need to change the course of your argument.

A word such as 'remote' is easy to decode with a little common sense. But sometimes you will be working at a question that turns on a more specialised term. For instance:

In what sense are 'The Rime of the Ancient Mariner' and 'Kubla Khan' works of 'pure imagination'?

or

Write an essay on Keats's qualities as a narrative poet.

In these cases your answer will depend substantially on how you under-stand 'imagination' and 'narrative', terms that have acquired extra layers of meaning in literary discourse. This book has been designed to help you with some of those terms, but its coverage is not comprehensive. You will need to refer to a book such as John Peck and Martin Coyle's *Literary Terms and Criticism* (in the same series as the present book), which provides an up-to-date introduction to the vocabulary of literary criticism. You need to be able to define with some confidence common labels such as 'ballad', 'imagery' and 'allegory' if your essay is not to wobble perilously under the weight of its own uncertainties.

YOUR ANSWER

The methods outlined in the earlier chapters of this book for reading lyric and narrative poetry were designed to help you mine the raw materials so that you can construct your own answers, but they will not build them for you. What you need to do next is to assemble that raw material and then sift and mould it so that it meets the particular demands of the question you have chosen. How do you do that?

The usual shape of an essay is a sequence of paragraphs, each one making a point that contributes to your case and moves your argument along towards a final answer. This is sometimes quite difficult to do. You may have had the experience of writing an essay that gets stuck in a repetitive groove with each paragraph adding another example but not actually advancing your response in any detectable way, so that the essay tends to drift to a lame stop when you run out of examples rather than when your thesis is logically complete.

There are various ways round this common difficulty. Here are some suggestions for enabling an essay to grow so that it is not dull to look at and it does keep reaching on towards its conclusion.

I   Work with the order in which the poems you are talking about were first written

You will be aware that what you think and believe today is in some ways, trivial or profound, different from what you thought and believed ten years ago. (If not, you should check to see if you are still alive.) As a result of a decade of experience, you will almost certainly have at least marginally different views on subjects as diverse as the cheapest place to buy decent potatoes and how best to cope with feelings of loss. Poets change in the same ways as the rest of us do. In this book, we have seen that the Blake who etched *Songs of Innocence* in 1789 had shifted his vision by 1794 when he came to add *Songs of Experience*, and as early as the autumn of 1819 Keats had developed beyond some of the ideas he had expressed in the spring of the same year. Uniform consistency is something to be hoped for in school custard but not to be expected of mobile and growing human beings.

These processes of change will mean that you can be faced with a statement in a question which you might feel is true enough of one stage in a writer's development but not of another. For example:

> 'His practice contradicts his theories.' Is this a just comment on Wordsworth's poetry?

or

> 'Keats understood better than most poets what subject matter is appropriate for poetry.' Discuss.

You might want to show that Wordsworth or Keats or whoever was closer to the position outlined in the question at one point in his career than at others. So a working sense of the chronology of the poems you intend to talk about will give your essay a natural shape and momentum.

2 Organise your answer around two or more different responses to the question

There is common agreement amongst literary critics that Blake was born on 28 November 1757, but that is about as far as common agreement on Blake extends, and indeed some critics would argue that the date of Blake's birth is of interest only to literary historians, not literary critics. The basis for this disagreement is plain enough. Part at least of the reason why a writer bothers to write at all is the conviction that something needs saying and that he or she is the one to say it. And, when later we pick up the resulting work and read it, it will, if it is any good at all, mobilise, stimulate, enhance or challenge our deepest convictions about life and its point. And about those things, in a multi-cultural, class-divided and changing society such as our own there is no consensus. A poem that delights and touches a feminist might strike a bricklayer as obscure and a parson as obscene. Granted their presuppositions, all three of them could be right.

If that is true, what follows for the essay writer? It suggests that you need to start by seeking out opinions from more than one source. Draw on your own reading of the text. Listen to others. Read some more in the library. Talk to someone about the text. Go back to it and think again. The resulting essay, however, should *not* be some sort of liberal swamp – an answer that see-saws back and forth between 'on the one hand' and 'on the other' till you reach the limp conclusion that it would be a funny old world if we all agreed. Rather, what you should aim for is to strengthen, clarify or modify your own ideas so that you can work towards a statement of them that is able to take on board some views, take account of some and resist some. Arguing your case against possible alternatives gives that case a sharpness and specificity it would lack if simply offered in a vacuum. After all, any reading of a poem denies at least by implication any other reading; sometimes it helps you and your reader to investigate those implications rather than slip silently past them and hope no one notices.

3   Work out your answer and assemble the evidence that led you to it

The problem with the advice that I have just offered is that, if you are not careful, your essay may end up as a vociferous exchange of opinion that gets no one anywhere. The feminist throws things at the bricklayer and the parson tries vainly to get in the way, but nobody learns anything and somebody usually gets hurt. You can avoid this by providing evidence for your opinion. That not only helps your argument to progress but also allows for rational discussion and response. If you have arrived at a set of convictions about a text, show how you got there and lay out the evidence that helped form your conclusions. The most obvious means of doing this is by quoting from the text in question as support for your argument. This stops you repeating what might sound like hazy beliefs about the poem and instead you actually go to work on the poem.

Counselling students to quote is not exactly stunningly original advice and it is something that everyone does from time to time. But using quotes effectively is a skill that needs to be learned and to that end I would offer the following four suggestions.

(a)   Only use a quotation to substantiate a part of your argument

In other words, don't use a quotation as an unconscious way of signalling to the reader that you haven't much to say about the poem but at least you can copy bits of it out of the book. A quotation needs to sustain an argument, not to serve as a substitute for one.

(b) Make your quotations as brief as possible

I say this not just because it is a brain-rotting waste of time to learn long quotations for an examination, although it certainly is that. Quotations need to be kept short – sometimes a phrase or even a word, usually two or three lines at most – because longer quotations will inevitably raise more issues than you will have time and space to deal with in an examination essay.

(c) Quotations don't speak for themselves – they need help

You might be writing about Blake's 'The Chimney Sweeper' from *Songs of Experience* and be tempted to say something like this: 'The poem ends very powerfully as the child describes his parents that "are gone to praise God & his Priest & King, / Who make up a heaven of our misery".' But why do you think these lines are powerful? Because of the subversive suggestion that the combined authority of the deity, priesthood and the monarchy is used to sanction the exploitation of children? Because of the alliterative emphasis of *gone/God, praise/Priest, make-up/misery*? Because of the brutal paradox of offering praise to the originators of misery? Because the parents have smugly departed to do their praising and left their child to his own unhappy devices? Because of the possibility of an ironic play on words, *make up* meaning both 'construct' and 'tell lies about'? You need to spell some of these things out rather than hope that the reader can guess them. Make a point of turning back on a quotation after you have completed it to work on its terms. After all, you have chosen it from the whole body of the text because it said something that struck you as having particular relevance to your case. Indicate that particular relevance; your readers won't know what it is unless you tell them.

(d) Make sure you quote correctly

Poets care about words. We have seen in this book that looking carefully at the words they choose and the way they combine them can help us to say substantial things about what they wrote. 'The Rime of the Ancient Mariner' is a poem about a man who kills an albatross, but the language Coleridge uses makes the text rather more than just a piece of propaganda for the Royal Society for the Protection of Birds. So in discussing that or indeed any poem it is important that you get the words right when you quote. You can sink a skilfully launched argument about Keats's 'To Autumn' by announcing that the last line is 'And gathering swallows titter in the skies'.

CONCLUSION

This book has aimed to help you read Romantic poetry and then write about it. I would summarise the essay-writing advice in this chapter as follows.

1 Read the poems carefully, using the methods outlined in the body of the book to provide you with your own ideas and responses.
2 When you set about writing an essay and shaping those ideas and responses into an answer, begin by interrogating if necessary some of the key terms in the question so that both you and your reader know where you are going.
3 Structure your answer as simply as possible in a series of paragraphs, each making a point that advances your case. There are various ways of moving your case forward – for example, by working with the chronology of the author's career, by examining different responses offered by different readers and by analysing brief quotations to provide specific and accumulating evidence.

A final thought. Romantic poetry is still worth reading after two hundred years because it is poetry written by people reacting with delight and terror, fascination and anger to the way the society we still inhabit was being violently re-created by a series of wars and political and social revolutions. Their poetry is about how they coped with that, how they sought to control it and how they realigned their lives in the light of it. Read as voraciously and as imaginatively and as thoughtfully as you can so that you can touch and share some of that excitement and horror. Above all, avoid romanticising Romantic poetry. It is poetry about how your world was smashed, distorted, expropriated, defended, remade and agonised over. When you begin to see and feel that, you won't need advice from anyone about how to write about it.

FURTHER READING

INTRODUCTORY TEXTS

I Critical theory

BEFORE you get anywhere in literary studies you will need to work out some theory of what it is you are doing and why you are doing it. Otherwise it will rapidly become a pointless activity and a deeply dreary one too, because you will have no mechanisms for generating your own analyses but will be limited to uncertain repetition of other people's. As I mentioned in the last chapter, there is a basic reference book in this series, John Peck and Martin Coyle, *Literary Terms and Criticism* (1984), which explains the vocabulary of the subject, and there are many others such as the *Penguin Dictionary of Literary Terms and Literary Theory* (3rd edition, 1992), ed. J.A. Cuddon. There are plenty of anthologies of literary theory; you might start with the biggest because you are most likely to find something there that intrigues you and the biggest is probably Julie Rivkin and Michael Ryan (eds), *Literary Theory: An Anthology* (1998). Then there are the many surveys of modern developments in critical theory. Three of the most accessible are Raman Selden, *Practising Theory and Reading Literature* (1989), Peter Barry, *Beginning Theory: An Introduction to Literary and Cultural Theory* (1995) and Terry Eagleton, *Literary Theory: An Introduction* (2nd edition, 1996). Finally, when you are faced with the problem of turning your ideas into answers, I think you will find David B. Pirie's *How to Write Critical Essays* (1985) full of lively advice and assistance.

2 Historical context

I have emphasised the need to see literary texts in their historical context in order to make sense of them, and there are various books that will enrich your knowledge of the period. The two classic studies are Eric Hobsbawm's *The Age of Revolution 1789–1848* (1962) and E.P.

Thompson's *The Making of the English Working Class* (1968). Books that bring together selections from contemporary documents to help you build your own sense of the times are Merryn Williams (ed.), *Revolutions 1775–1830* (1971); Marilyn Butler (ed.), *Burke, Paine, Godwin and the Revolution Controversy* (1984); and Vivien Jones (ed.), *Women in the Eighteenth Century* (1990). In a crowded field, Linda Colley's theses in *Britons: Forging the Nation 1707–1837* (1992) offer provocative lines of enquiry for students of literature.

3 Literary context

There have been many introductions to Romantic literature, but you need to be wary of the older ones which are inevitably out of touch with both the scholarly discoveries and the revolutions in critical theory that have taken place in recent years. That said, the finest study I have come across remains Marilyn Butler's *Romantics, Rebels and Reactionaries: English Literature and its Background 1760–1830* (1981). The most recent is the massive *Oxford Companion to the Romantic Age: British Culture 1776–1832* (1999) ed. Iain McCalman, containing articles on everything from music to policing and from slavery to consumerism. Of many other books in the field, I have found that students seem to learn most from four in particular: Stuart Curran (ed.), *The Cambridge Companion to British Romanticism* (1993); Aidan Day, *Romanticism* (1996); W.G. Rowland (ed.), *Literature and the Marketplace: Romantic Writers and their Audiences in Great Britain and the United States* (1996); and E.P. Thompson, *The Romantics: England in a Revolutionary Age* (1997). I have tried to describe the radical culture of the early 1790s, which is referred to several times in this book, in an essay I contributed to a collection edited by John Lucas, *Writing and Radicalism* (1996). Finally, you will find much fuller critical bibliographies than I have space for here covering all the major writers of the period in Michael J. O'Neill (ed.), *Literature of the Romantic Period: A Bibliographical Guide* (1998).

BLAKE

I Editions

Most students working for an examination will have no choice about the edition they use. In the chapter on Blake I worked from Jacob

Bronowski's selection entitled *Blake: Poems and Letters* (1958) simply because it is one I have used for years but there are many more recent ones on the market. The problem with nearly all of them is that, in order to remain reasonably cheap, they exclude Blake's illuminations which are an important part of his work. You can find these in Geoffrey Keynes's paperback edition of *William Blake: Songs of Innocence and of Experience* (1970). The standard complete editions of Blake, both with very useful notes, are Alicia Ostriker (ed.), *William Blake: The Complete Poems* (1977) and David Erdman (ed.), *The Complete Poetry and Prose of William Blake* (1988).

2 Criticism

The Macmillan *Casebook* series is always worth consulting because each volume collects both contemporary responses and more recent views: the one on *Songs of Innocence and of Experience* is edited by Margaret Bottrall (1970). There are two good books that will help you make sense of Blake's illuminations: they are W.J.T. Mitchell's *Blake's Composite Art: A Study of the Illuminated Poetry* (1978) and J. Viscomi's *Blake and the Idea of the Book* (1993). The 1990s was a great decade for Blake studies and, of many texts published in that decade, I learnt most from three: Jonathan Mee, *Dangerous Enthusiasm: William Blake and the Culture of Radicalism in the 1790s* (1992); E.P. Thompson, *Witness Against the Beast: William Blake and the Moral Law* (1993); and Helen Bruder, *William Blake and the Daughters of Albion* (1997). The best of recent critical essays are collected in John Lucas (ed.), *William Blake* (1998) and in Steve Clark and David Worrall (eds), *Blake in the Nineties* (1999). The most recent biography is Peter Ackroyd's *Blake* (1995).

WORDSWORTH

1 Editions

When quoting 'Lines Written in Early Spring' in Chapter 3, I used the five-volume *Poetical Works of William Wordsworth*, ed. E. de Selincourt and H. Darbishire (1940–49). But if you are looking for more manageable texts, try R.L. Brett and A.R. Jones (eds), *Lyrical Ballads* (1963) because that has Wordsworth's 1798 Advertisement and 1800 Preface as well as ample notes and so I worked with that when discussing 'Tintern

Abbey'. Our understanding of the composition of *The Prelude* changed
in the last quarter of the twentieth century; the edition that incorpo-
rates that knowledge most conveniently is Jonathan Wordsworth (ed.),
The Prelude: The Four Texts (1798, 1799, 1805, 1850) (1995).

2   Criticism

If you want to learn more about Wordsworth's life, then the definitive
biography is Stephen Gill's *William Wordsworth: A Life* (1989) which you
can supplement with the more recent Kenneth R. Johnston, *The Hidden
Wordsworth: Poet, Lover, Rebel, Spy* (1998). Nicholas Roe, *Wordsworth and
Coleridge: The Radical Years* (1988) is wonderfully informative on the
political contexts of the decade leading up to the *Lyrical Ballads*, while
Richard Cronin (ed.), *1798: The Year of the 'Lyrical Ballads'* (1998)
gathers together essays that re-read that text in the light of its
contemporary moment. The *New Casebook* is John Williams (ed.),
Wordsworth (1993). Mary Jacobus is the most theoretically astute
Wordsworth critic, and there is a large amount of intelligent information in her *Tradition and Experiment in Wordsworth's 'Lyrical Ballads'*
(1976) and *Romanticism, Writing and Sexual Difference: Essays on 'The
Prelude'* (1989).

COLERIDGE

1   Editions

The edition I used for the Coleridge poems discussed in Chapter 5 was
the Oxford Standard Authors text *Coleridge: Poetical Works*, ed. E.H.
Coleridge (1912). A more recent edition with helpful notes is William
Keach (ed.), *Coleridge: The Complete Poems* (1997).

2   Criticism

Further reading on Coleridge these days ought to begin with Richard
Holmes. First his concise *Coleridge* (1982), which includes a brief biography, and then the much fuller *Coleridge: Early Visions* (1989) and

Coleridge: Darker Reflections (1998). To this may be added J.R. de J. Jackson (ed.), *Coleridge: The Critical Heritage* (1970), which collects reviews and essays on Coleridge by his contemporaries, and the *New Casebook* ed. Peter J. Kitson, *Coleridge, Keats and Shelley* (1996). There are two stimulatingly different and historically informed readings of Coleridge in the period covered by Chapter 5 in Nicholas Roe, *Wordsworth and Coleridge: The Radical Years* (1988) and, for a more disillusioned view, in E.P. Thompson, *The Romantics: England in a Revolutionary Age* (1997). Also making sense of Coleridge in a historical context is Kelvin Everest, *Coleridge's Secret Ministry: The Context of the Conversation Poems 1795–1798* (1979).

KEATS

I Editions

My source for the poems I discussed in Chapter 6 was H.W. Garrod (ed.), *Keats: Poetical Works* (1956). John Barnard (ed.), *Keats: The Complete Poems* (3rd edition, 1988) is very useful for students because it has full notes.

2 Criticism

The standard life of Keats is now Andrew Motion's *Keats* (1997). I used *The Letters of John Keats*, ed. Hyder E. Rollins (2 volumes, 1958) for the letters I quoted in Chapter 6; this or the paperback selection edited by Robert Gittings, *Letters of John Keats* (1970), is a marvellous source of ideas and excitement about Keats and his work supplied by the poet himself. The *Casebooks* are *Keats: The Odes*, edited by G.S. Fraser (1971) and *Keats: The Narrative Poems*, ed. John Spencer Hill (1983); this can be supplemented with the *New Casebook* ed. Peter J. Kitson, *Coleridge, Keats and Shelley* (1996) and with Helen Vendler's *The Odes of John Keats* (1983). Of recent work on Keats, I would recommend starting with two books by Nicholas Roe: his edited collection *Keats and History* (1995) gathers together recent feminist and historicist criticism and his book *John Keats and the Culture of Dissent* (1997) re-reads the poetry by pushing it close up against a detailed realisation of Keats's life.

WOMEN'S POETRY

1 Editions

There are facsimile editions becoming available of texts such as Mary Robinson's 1791 *Poems* and her 1799 *A Letter to the Women of England, on the Injustice of Mental Subordination*, published by Woodstock Books, and there are also some complete editions such as Stuart Curran's *The Poems of Charlotte Smith* (1993) and William McCarthy and Elizabeth Craft's *The Poems of Anna Laetitia Barbauld* (1994). But all of these books tend to be expensive and are aimed primarily at scholars and at libraries. At the moment of writing I am not aware of any cheap paperback editions of individual women Romantic poets. I am sure that situation will change in the next few years. Till then most students will work with one of the many anthologies which have appeared since Roger Lonsdale's pioneering *Eighteenth-Century Women Poets* (1989) which I have used for the poems discussed in Chapter 7. The most helpful of such anthologies I have found to be Jennifer Breen (ed.), *Women Romantic Poets 1785–1832* (1992), Andrew Ashfield (ed.), *Romantic Women Poets 1770–1838* (1995) and Duncan Wu (ed.), *Romantic Women Poets* (1997).

2 Criticism

Compared to the sagging shelves full of work on the four men discussed in this book, there is as yet little work done on Romantic women poets. In some ways this is a help because students are encouraged to think and write freely about those poets without an inhibiting sense of the libraries full of scholarship that they should read before they dare open their mouths. That said, preliminary information is obviously helpful and I have learnt most about Elizabeth Hands from Donna Landry, *The Muses of Resistance: Laboring-Class Women's Poetry in Britain 1739–1796* (1990) and about Mary Robinson from some asides in Stuart Curran's *The Cambridge Companion to British Romanticism* (1993). There is a growing body of feminist criticism which rethinks Romanticism in the light of the work of previously ignored women writers. The most exciting and challenging criticism of this sort I have found to be (in chronological order of publication): Margaret Homans, *Women Writers and Poetic Identity: Dorothy Wordsworth, Emily Brontë and Emily Dickinson* (1980); Ann Mellor (ed.), *Romanticism and Feminism* (1988); Marlon Ross, *The Contours of Masculine Desire: Romanticism and the Rise of Women's Poetry*

(1989); Sylvia Myers, *The Bluestocking Circle: Women, Friendship and the Life of the Mind in Eighteenth Century England* (1990); Gary Kelly, *Women, Writing and Revolution* (1993); Ann Mellor, *Romanticism and Gender* (1993); Mary Favret and Nicola Watson (eds), *At the Limits of Romanticism: Essays in Feminist and Materialist Criticism* (1994); and Elizabeth Fay, *A Feminist Introduction to Romanticism* (1998). The critical bibliography edited by Michael O'Neill, *Literature of the Romantic Period: A Bibliographical Guide* (1998) has a particularly useful section by Jennifer Breen entitled 'Women Poets of the Romantic Period'.

INDEX